COUNTRY
CHURCHES
of

ENGLAND SCOTLAND AND WALES
A GUIDE AND GAZETTEER

COUNTRY CHURCHES

of

ENGLAND SCOTLAND AND WALES
A GUIDE AND GAZETTEER

GEOFFREY YOUNG

CHANCELLOR
PRESS

First published in 1991 by George Philip Limited
59 Grosvenor Street, London W1X 9DA

This edition published 2003 by Chancellor Press,
an imprint of Bounty Books, a division of
Octopus Publishing Group Ltd,
2-4 Heron Quays, London E14 4JP

British Library Cataloguing in Publication Data

Young, Geoffrey, *1936*–
  Country churches of England, Scotland and Wales.
  1. Great Britain. Parish churches – Visitors'
  guides
  I. Title
  914.104859

ISBN 0-7537-0642-3

Page design Janette Widdows
Typeset by BAS Printers Limited,
Over Wallop, Hampshire, Great Britain
Printed and bound in Hong Kong

———————◆———————

Title-page illustration *The church at Staunton Harold, founded in 1653*

Contents

◆

Introduction

———◆———

The country churches that we inherit are amongst the most varied of all. But they are not simply a library of changing architectural styles. They also reflect – and this is their fascination – changes in the lives, attitudes and opinions of ordinary people through the centuries.

Sometimes these changes have been speedy and cataclysmic. More usually, though, they have taken place across generations and have perhaps been scarcely noticed by those alive at the time. And this is why we, through the village church, can examine the past from a privileged viewpoint.

We can piece together the clues given by the remaining fragments of wall paintings or old window glass. Tombs and memorials speak to us in their own way. We can decipher the seemingly endless rearrangements to the insides of even small churches as witnessed by scars and mauls on pillars, walls and floors. These resulted not from the whims of architects but from changes in the way the villagers used the church. And some of these past uses may surprise us – churches were regular refuges from flood and fire or even border marauders, and armour was frequently stored in them. They were also used for village feasts accompanied by singing and dancing. Even some common turns of phrase we take for granted today are rooted in the village church, such as 'going to the wall' (explained on page 53) and 'shady characters' (those of dubious morals perhaps, who were buried in the least favoured, shaded part of the churchyard north of the church).

So, in this fresh look at British country churches, we also hope to give you a deep insight into the past.

The book is organized in the following way:

Origins Sixteen brief sections trace the development of church architecture, linked to the religious and social uses of the country church over the centuries.
Gazetteer An alphabetical list of 100 outstanding churches to visit throughout England, Scotland and Wales. As far as possible, these have been chosen to offer the reader a choice of ages, styles and other points of interest within a Sunday drive. (A special section on churches in Scotland explains in greater detail how

these have followed a different path of development to the rest of Britain, with examples listed alphabetically.)

Maps Each of the churches described in the gazetteer is marked in red on one or more of the four preceding regional maps on pages 56–9. Principal roads, towns and county boundaries are also shown to assist in pinpointing each church's precise location. In addition, six of the entries in the gazetteer have been specially selected as a 'Guided Tour', in which the reader is taken on a fascinating in-depth visit around the church; these six churches are denoted by red capital letters on the regional maps.

Glossary A concise explanation of architectural terms.

Index This can be used to find points of history, politics, church administration or social use which are elaborated in the 16 introductory sections and in some of the gazetteer entries. With the index you can find your way to explanations of the difference between a vicar and a rector, plus such terms as tithes, Reformation and Puritan. The index will also lead you to descriptions of features such as wall paintings and misericords.

Architectural Time Chart

There is an understandable overlap of these dates, since innovations in architecture usually spread by diffusion.

600–1066	Saxon (pre-Conquest Romanesque)
1066–1160	Norman (Romanesque)
1160–1200	Transitional
1200–1280	Early English (Early Gothic)
1280–1350	Decorated (High Gothic)
1350–1550	Perpendicular (Late Gothic) merging into Tudor
1550–1660	The Reformation
1603–1689	Stuart kings
1689–1833	Hanoverians (William and Mary, Anne, the Georges)
1830–1900	Gothic Revival (Victorian)

} some classical revival

I
Origins

Christianity became the official religion of the Roman Empire in AD 313. But the withdrawal of the Roman legions from Britain by AD 425 left the islands open to invasion, and pagan 'Saxons' (Angles, Saxons and Jutes) pushed the young religion back. It seems to have survived only in the West Country, parts of the North (Lindisfarne became one stronghold) and also in Ireland, which was distanced from the turmoil. This original 'Celtic' Church, as might have been found at Glastonbury (Somerset) or Tintagel (Cornwall) in the 6th century, was organized from small monastic settlements. These were little more than a cluster of huts surrounding a tiny, perhaps wooden chapel, from which the priests travelled to preach under an open sky.

Christianity triumphant had to await the arrival of St Augustine's mission in Kent in AD 597. Its success was such that its influence had reached the far north within 30 years, and Christianity became adopted by many English rulers. More permanent churches were built, often mimicking Romano-British features, such as the tile arches at BRIXWORTH (Northamptonshire). Although bruised by the onslaughts of Danish and Norwegian Vikings, the religion survived. King Alfred's policy of converting the Danish Vikings, and his victory over them at EDINGTON (Wiltshire) in AD 878, led eventually to a revival of 'Saxon' church building. BREAMORE (Hampshire) is a fine example. Many churches surviving from this period were 'minsters', a term derived from the word monastery. They were religious centres serving the great Saxon estates, and were politically important too, for literate clerics would help with administration. A number of them have maintained their key status with the Saxon minster being rebuilt as the cathedral we see today – York Minster (which dates from 1220) is one of those that keeps its old title. Many, however, can be visited which are barely changed: for example, WORTH (West Sussex) and WING (Buckinghamshire).

Minsters are best thought of as 'mother churches'. From them the monks or clerics journeyed on missionary work in their neighbourhood, often preaching at a cross of stone or wood erected at the centre of a settlement. The newly devout *thegn* (local lord) of a small estate might erect a simple wooden 'field church' or chapel, perhaps associated with his Hall, and for which he would appoint his

Left *A 'Celtic' cross memorial in the churchyard at Blisland in Cornwall*

own priest. Unlike a minster, however, such a church did not have a consecrated burial ground.

From these humbler estates evolved the parishes, the 'field church' being the forerunner of the parish church. Throughout the Middle Ages, the 'lord of the manor', whether as an individual or (as became increasingly common) in the form of a nearby religious house, continued to appoint the parish priest. Where they exist, Saxon land charters can sometimes show that today's parish boundary dates back to that time, as at WINTERBOURNE BASSETT (Wiltshire).

After the Norman Conquest of 1066, churches were extended or rebuilt in stone, or in wood as at LOWER PEOVER (Cheshire). Many new churches were built, too. The money needed to pay for this extensive building programme and the church's dictatorial role came from the tithes, which amounted to a tenth of the parish produce. In time the parishioners were made responsible for the maintenance of the nave, and the tithes were used only to maintain the chancel. The tithes helped decide the size of the parish. Where settlements were small, poor and scattered, a parish might include many villages or hamlets spread over a large area; in richer areas, just one.

A system of clergy evolved. A rector had the right to the church income, but in medieval times, the main tithes of corn, hay and wool and the income from the 'glebe' or church land were usually taken by a monastery; the arrangement at DALMENY (Lothian) is just one example of this system. The abbot might appoint a vicar on a small salary, or a rector. He was often an absentee career man, in the service of bishop or baron, who in turn appointed his own vicar as a curate (assistant). The curate might make up his salary from lesser tithes and burial and other fees. There were also chaplains who scraped a living from services in *chantries* (usually side chapels built by rich families who had paid for prayers to be said for their souls). At the bottom of the hierarchy were the clerks.

The location of churches can give an indication of their history. Being linked originally with the lord of the manor, many country churches stand near the manor house. Others were often built where the preaching crosses had stood; sites perhaps originally chosen because they were already sacred to non-Christians. The parish of BLISLAND (Cornwall) has pagan stones carved later with crosses. High spots were often places of pagan worship: BRENTOR (Devon) is a church perched on an eyrie, and HOLME UPON SPALDING MOOR (Humberside) stands alone on a hill. Such churches are often solitary, but many churches which are now isolated stand at the sites of abandoned villages; neither STANFORD ON AVON (Northamptonshire) nor SALL (Norfolk) can really claim a village today. Some churchyards contain two churches, as at SWAFFHAM PRIOR (Cambridgeshire); they served two parishes but were built to share an island of better bedrock.

OTHER CHURCHES

Two parish churches which retain the old title 'minster' are Beverley Minster (Humberside) and Wimborne Minster (Dorset). Churches are found beside the manor house at Stokesay (Shropshire), Brympton d'Evercy (Somerset) and Chastleton (Oxfordshire). Those on pre-Christian religious sites include Rudston (Humberside) with a great standing stone in its churchyard. Knowlton (Dorset) lies within the banks of a New Stone Age ritual henge. Saxon crosses can be seen in the churchyards of Bewcastle (Cumbria) and Bakewell (Derbyshire). Another church on a high point is Breedon on the Hill (Leicestershire). There are many solitary churches to be seen, some in good order – Sandon (Staffordshire) is maintained by the stately home nearby – and some derelict, such as Egmere (Norfolk).

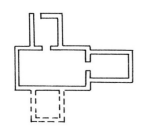

VARIETY OF SAXON CHURCH PLAN

SET OF PAIRED WINDOWS

SAXON STONE FONT

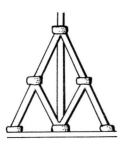

'MATCHSTICK' DECORATION

SAXON

Britain's surviving Saxon churches fall into two groups. The first consists of the 'Celtic' churches in western areas, such as Wales and Somerset, and the North, which were built in the 7th and early 8th centuries and which survived the Viking invasions. Wooden Celtic churches have rotted away, but a few stone-and-rubble churches remain: buildings with a tall, narrow nave leading through an arched opening to a square-ended chancel or sanctuary, as at ESCOMB (County Durham). St Augustine's mission spreading from Kent early in the 7th century brought churches of a grander 'basilican' design based on the Roman law court: a broad nave, perhaps with a row of rooms at each side, with an apse – a sanctuary with a curved end wall – at the eastern end. (In the original Roman basilica, the magistrate would have sat here flanked by advisers.)

The rivalry between the two Churches was not simply architectural, for the Celtic Church had been isolated from Rome for some time. Its simple hierarchy lacked bishops, and it also disputed such significant details as the date of Easter in the Church calendar. Agreement reached at the Synod of Whitby in AD 664 favoured the newcomers, and their basilican plan tended to influence church building in many areas around this time. BRIXWORTH (Northamptonshire), possibly dating from AD 680, has some basilican features. But the square-ended style, as can be seen at BRADFORD ON AVON (Wiltshire), remained dominant in Wessex and the square-ended church eventually became the norm in Britain.

Then came troubled centuries of Norwegian and Danish Viking raids and settlement. But a new age of church building appears to have begun in the 10th century. Most Saxon churches which are still standing date from these later times, including those at BREAMORE (Hampshire), WING (Buckinghamshire) and WORTH (West Sussex). Fragments of distinctive red tile suggest that the rubble and stone were often looted from a nearby Roman villa.

One feature fairly typical of churches of this period was a facing pair of *porticus*, low side chapels, attached where the nave and chancel met, to form a 'crossing', with a tower above. These porticus have usually disappeared, but one remains at BREAMORE. Porticus were later to evolve into transepts framed by arches, but in these early days the entrances to the porticus from the crossing were like that to the sanctuary – simply a small arched doorway piercing the wall. At STOW (Lincolnshire), completed just before the Norman Conquest, the porticus are as high as the nave – another step towards true transepts. Although little is known about Saxon liturgy, the crossing probably contained the great altar and was thus the ritual focus of the church.

There might also be porticus as part of a porch at the west end of the nave, making a *narthex*. It was here that those converted but not yet baptized (and so forbidden to enter the church) could be instructed.

These stone-and-rubble churches were minsters, or mother churches, but the

The atmospheric interior of the church of St Lawrence at Bradford on Avon

The polygonal apse at Wing, which dates from the 10th century

Saxons were adept builders in wood, and many lesser 'field churches' were probably made of timber or half-timbered, the areas between the beams filled with daub. At GREENSTED (Essex) a nave wall of split oak logs survives.

The Saxons built towers above the crossing, as at BREAMORE, or at the west end. They often have a simple beauty. Pilaster strips, making a 'matchstick' decoration, perhaps in imitation of timbering, are often featured. SOMPTING (West Sussex) keeps its original four-gabled 'helm' cap.

Although the Normans tended to rebuild important churches from the foundations up, there are still over 200 churches which are partly or largely Saxon. So distinctive is Saxon work that even a fragment is immediately recognizable. The rubble walls are sometimes strengthened by zigzagging or *herring-boning* the pieces; the corners are strengthened with massive *long-and-short work* (a type of *quoining*) – long stones on end between flat ones which extended through the wall. Pilasters, even if more for ornament, were also for strengthening. Windows are small, and often at the centre of the wall which is splayed or cut back at each side to allow more light and air in, without creating draughts. They usually have a triangular or a semicircular head (sometimes carved out of a single piece of stone). Windows are often paired, and sometimes separated by a cylindrical shaft, which may have been turned on a lathe – an echo of woodworking tradition. Doorways are usually narrow. Arches may be neatly masoned, but many are only roughly finished.

Little Saxon decoration or sculpture remains, compared with Norman and later times, but what does remain gives us some insight into the Saxon heart: the Christ in Majesty at BARNACK (Cambridgeshire) is moving, as is the famous DEERHURST (Gloucestershire) angel, while INGLESHAM (Wiltshire) has a fine Saxon carving of the Virgin and Child.

NORMAN

Norman architecture (which is also known as English Romanesque) did not originate in Normandy, but is an adapted version of the Romanesque style brought to Britain by the Normans. With wealth looted from the Saxon English, the Norman bishops set about rebuilding the more important cathedrals and minsters soon after their invasion in 1066.

It was not until the following century that the lesser churches were enlarged, or rebuilt in stone instead of wood. Many of the first Norman country churches were simple in plan: KILPECK (Hereford and Worcester) remains unaltered, consisting of a nave and chancel with a curved sanctuary apse at its east end. HALES (Norfolk) has simple charm, with its plain nave, tiny apsed chancel, thatched

OTHER CHURCHES

St Peter's near Bradwell on Sea (Essex) is an early church, dating to about AD 650. Repton (Derbyshire) has a fine Saxon crypt. Saxon towers are seen at Appleton-le-Street (North Yorkshire), Earls Barton (Northamptonshire) and Barton on Humber (Humberside); the last two of these also have 'matchstick' decoration. Round towers include Herringfleet (Suffolk) and Bessingham (Norfolk). At Monkwearmouth (County Durham) the tall tower (dated to around AD 900, and possibly Britain's oldest) was raised on a two-storeyed porch. Great Paxton (Cambridgeshire) and Heysham (Lancashire) also have some Saxon features. There is a complete Saxon sundial, dated *c.* 1060, at Kirkdale (North Yorkshire).

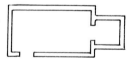

A NORMAN CHURCH PLAN

Right *St Mary's crypt at Lastingham, which has remained virtually unchanged since Norman times*

The church tower at Penmon retains its original Norman pyramid roof

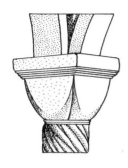

CUSHION CAPITAL

ROUND-HEADED NORMAN WINDOW

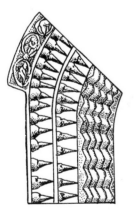

BEAKHEAD MOULDING

roof and round tower. CULBONE (Somerset), the smallest parish church in England, retains a simple feel despite later alterations.

Norman churches are as distinctive as Saxon churches. A typical Norman church was squat, with massive walls. The most imposing churches were cruciform, with side transepts, as at MELBOURNE (Derbyshire). This allowed room for more altars (and thus more priests, as each priest had to say mass daily, but no altar could be used more than once a day). The nave was sometimes aisled, perhaps to create processional ways which avoided the crowds of the standing congregation. Aisles such as those at MELBOURNE distanced the side windows, so a *clerestory* was added: a row of windows inserted into the upper wall of the nave above the height of the side aisles to let more light into the main body of the church.

An arcade between the nave and the side aisle, carrying the wall, was constructed with *piers* of rubble packed within axe-cut facing stones. Such piers were of a weak construction, and so needed to be built thick to support the wall and roof above. The piers were round (or later octagonal).

To give greater support for the springing of the arch, the top of the pillar was enlarged as a 'capital', on which sat a flat, square *abacus* carrying the arch. The arch was semicircular and neatly built of cut blocks of stone. As the wall was thick, the arch might be recessed in bands, known as *orders*, which were often highly decorated.

Doorways and windows could be recessed in the same way as arches. Windows were single rather than double (which was a Saxon feature), but were still small and narrow. They are often splayed inside, with the opening flush with the outside wall.

The Normans also began to experiment with more complex types of vaulting, such as that remaining in the chancel at WARKWORTH (Northumberland) and also (powerfully) in the crypt at LASTINGHAM (North Yorkshire).

The ambitious Normans built towers which were often decorated. Some of those which remain are at the west end of the church, others placed more centrally over the crossing. Some were later capped by spires, but at PENMON (Gwynedd) the original squat pyramid cap remains. At IFFLEY (Oxfordshire), the tower is central, even though the church lacks transepts. The massive weight of such a central tower was no longer supported on walls pierced with openings in the Saxon fashion, but spread down through semicircular arches to thick piers of rubble and masonry at the four corners. The Normans' ambition was not always matched by architectural skill and most Norman towers fell within a century or two, which is why we see so many Gothic towers today.

Exuberance was also expressed in the large quantities of axe-cut Norman decoration, usually including a *chevron* (zigzag) pattern. The recessed orders on doorways provided an ideal place for sculpture. KILPECK has foliage, animals and figures carved on its main entrance. A very popular motif from about 1140 was

The south doorway at Kilpeck is famous for its amazing decoration

a chain of *beakheads*, birds, animals or monsters biting a *roll moulding* (a moulding with a semicircular profile, running round the door, arch or window) as at IFFLEY. The *tympanum* (the semicircular panel over a door lintel) could have a sculpted scene such as Christ in Majesty. The outside walls could have *string courses* (horizontal bands projecting from the wall) or *blind arcades* (arcades attached to the wall as a decorative motif), and the *corbels* (little stone blocks projecting from the wall acting as brackets) supporting the roof could be carved with faces, animals or figures. Inside, the arcades, vaulting ribs, windows and chancel arch could also be richly decorated, as at IFFLEY. Capitals on arches could be plain 'cushion' capitals (a cube with its bottom angles rounded down to a circle), scalloped, fluted, or carved with foliage, animals or mythical beasts.

There is more than one origin for the scrapbook of images which adorn the outside of a Norman church such as KILPECK. Some undoubtedly were a kind of shorthand, a code for Christian values – the hare and the hound foresaking their natural emnity, for example. But others are almost certainly descended directly from pre-Roman beliefs and imagery.

Norman fonts were often carved with similar subject-matter, and come in a variety of shapes. DORCHESTER (Oxfordshire) has a rare example of a lead font, while that at YOULGREAVE (Derbyshire) is unique in that it has a second, smaller stoup beside the main bowl.

Norman builders left us some church oddities. One is at COMPTON (Surrey), where there is a two-storeyed sanctuary at the east end, the only one in Europe. Also unusual are the round-naved, knight-order churches such as the Hospitaller church at LITTLE MAPLESTEAD (Essex), which was modelled on Jerusalem's Holy Sepulchre.

OTHER CHURCHES
Bossall (North Yorkshire), Adel (West Yorkshire) and Little Barrington (Gloucestershire) are cruciform churches. There are splendid towers at Brayton (North Yorkshire) and Castor (Cambridgeshire), and round towers, of Norman date but local Saxon tradition, at Little Saxham (Suffolk) and Great Leigh (Essex). Chancel arches were a feature of Norman churches – the massive arch at Tickencote (Leicestershire) is warped by its own weight. Barfreston (Kent) and Dinton (Buckinghamshire) have magnificent doorways; a wooden door survives at Staplehurst (Kent). There are fine Norman fonts at Eardisley and Castle Frome (both in Hereford and Worcester).

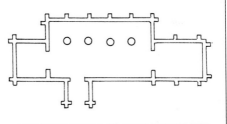

A TRANSITIONAL OR EARLY ENGLISH
CHURCH PLAN

GOTHIC: TRANSITIONAL AND EARLY ENGLISH

Conquest had suddenly imposed the Norman version of the Romanesque style in Britain, but the Gothic style developed gradually over 300 years. There was a period of transition when perhaps the new kind of pointed 'Early English' arch might spring from fat Norman pillars, as at SELBORNE (Hampshire). In many churches, such as GREAT BOOKHAM (Surrey), ST BRIAVELS (Gloucestershire) and WHITCHURCH CANONICORUM (Dorset), arcades of Norman and Transitional or Early English style exist side by side.

What evolved was another spirit, one that sought to glorify with lightness – as window space increased, filling the church with light and the arches pointed heavenwards. The term 'Gothic', with its echoes of barbarism, was coined later, in contempt, when people were heady with classicism. In the 19th century the three main periods of Gothic – Early, High and Late – were renamed Early English (*c.* 1200–80), Decorated (*c.* 1280–1350) and Perpendicular (*c.* 1350–1550). Early English was not restricted to England, whereas Perpendicular was, but the terms remain in use.

The dates attached to these three periods are not exact: remote, provincial areas tended to lag behind, and it could take several generations to change a building. Most churches show a mixture of styles.

With Gothic, building became a more skilful marriage of aesthetics and engineering. The major characteristic of Gothic is the 'pointed' arch. The French call it the *arc brisé*, a broken arch. By 'breaking' the semicircular Romanesque arch, the masons took a step forward.

The round arch is limiting. Saxon and Norman barrel and groin vaults could only reach the height of the semicircle, so a vault could only be half as high above the springing of the arch as it was wide. By using pointed arches to create the supporting skeleton which was then infilled with rubble and stone, a higher vault could be built. Also, the use of a pointed arch between the pillars in an arcade carried the weight of the wall more vertically down each pillar; hence the pillars (if well made) could be much thinner than their Norman predecessors. The slender, solid pillars were round or octagonal, and often adorned by slighter shafts, 'tied' to the main pillar by bonding rings. These shafts might be of Purbeck 'marble' – which is actually a hard, dark limestone. Later they merged to form multiple pillars (which are also known as *compound piers*). The walls of Gothic churches were also generally thinner, and a larger part of their weight passed down through the external buttressing, which developed eventually into that epitome of Gothic architecture – the flying buttress.

The pointed arch was also recognized as an inspiring design motif in its own right – rising up from the top of the pillar it carried the eye up with it. Although first seen in Durham Cathedral in the early 12th century, the real birth of Gothic style in Britain was with the building of the east end of Canterbury Cathedral from 1175 to 1184.

In the Early English period, country churches often had their chancels extended. The Victorians were to put their choirs here, but in the 13th century, humble churches did not have choirs. Another notable Early English addition might be a tower (perhaps to replace a Norman one which had fallen) – WEST WALTON (Norfolk) has a fine tower, separate from the church itself. Many of these towers were now capped by spires.

The first windows of the Early English style were *lancets* (very slim with pointed tops). These were simple, but could be impressive when ranked down the walls as at HALTWHISTLE (Northumberland), and their motif adds grandeur to the west front at FELMERSHAM (Bedfordshire). Lancets were also used for the

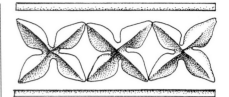

DOGTOOTH MOULDING

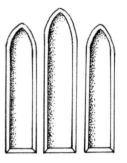

TRIPLE LANCET WINDOWS

Right *The west front of St Mary's at Felmersham, with its fine decoration*

graceful belfry openings of KETTON (Leicestershire), and the motif is echoed in the unusual triple chancel arch at WESTWELL (Kent).

The *dripstone* or *hood moulding*, the arched ledge that stops the rain dribbling down into the window and (as glass was still rare) into the building, could be extended to shield all the lancets in a group. The empty, stone 'plate' lying between the lancet points could then be cut through to make an extra window to let in more light. This new opening could be round or elaborated into an ornamental *trefoil* (three-lobed) or *quatrefoil* (four-lobed) opening. This is how 'plate tracery' was born – design born of opportunity. Tracery was to become increasingly elaborate as the next phase of the Gothic style developed.

Shadow and light are manipulated in the ornamentation of Early English arches. Some late Norman decoration developed further during this period: deeper-cut roll mouldings ran up the arches, and the old chevron ornament became, with deeper cutting, a pattern of hollowed-out four-cornered stars known as *dogtooth*. Another development was *nailhead*, a pattern of low pyramids.

In Early English sculpture, the hammer and chisel replaced the axe, and deep undercutting became possible. EATON BRAY (Bedfordshire) has good examples of deeply carved capitals. Two fairly typical Early English motifs were *waterleaf* and the more stylized *stiff-leaf*. Fonts, such as that at HIGH HALDEN (Kent), tended to be plainer than Norman ones. But extra decoration can be seen in the ornate scrolled ironwork of the doors, an example of which is at EATON BRAY. A chest of this period at ICKLINGHAM (Suffolk) has similar ironwork. The design of ironwork of this kind is a fitting companion for Early English stone carving.

GOTHIC: DECORATED

The Decorated style, the ornate high summer of Gothic, emerged gradually, but its end came more abruptly, after the Black Death struck just before 1350. Whole villages were emptied and forgotten, and perhaps the church remains in ruins as it does at Wharram Percy in North Yorkshire.

The Decorated style coincided with a time of national optimism under the later Plantagenets. Patron and mason alike seem to have become dissatisfied with simplicity, and confidently sought ever-increasing elaboration. There are a few entirely Decorated churches to be seen – PATRINGTON (Humberside) is one, while WINTERBOURNE BASSETT (Wiltshire), YAXLEY (Cambridgeshire) and DORCHESTER (Oxfordshire) have many features. But details can be found in many others.

The plan of the church had usually been adapted by now; aisles, transepts and chantry chapels were consistent features. The roofs might reflect this. The steep pitch of the nave roof meant that the additional aisle had to have a separate

OTHER CHURCHES

Transitional features are to be seen at New Shoreham (East Sussex), Avebury (Wiltshire), Faringdon (Oxfordshire) and Deeping St James (Lincolnshire). This last church has Gothic piers and Gothic roll mouldings on the arches, although the arches themselves are round. There are good Early English arcades at Slimbridge (Gloucestershire) and Uffington (Oxfordshire). Lancet windows in threes are seen at Stanton Harcourt (Oxfordshire), in fives at Chetwode (Buckinghamshire) and in a set of seven in the chancel of Ockham (Surrey). Simple circle plates are seen at Castor (Cambridgeshire) and quatrefoil plates at Edlesborough (Buckinghamshire) and Oundle (Northamptonshire).

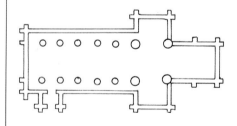

A DECORATED CHURCH PLAN

A fierce-looking gargoyle at St Mary's, Haddington

roof. Structural changes were accompanied by new forms of ornamentation; the outside buttressing had its own dead weight increased by pinnacles, which could be decorated with crockets. Gargoyles – waterspouts shaped as grotesque heads, people or monsters – became increasingly popular.

Seating now began to fill the nave, and the villagers might gather to hear a sermon given by a wandering friar. With this effective blocking of the nave, the aisles provided alternative routes for processions. Ornate *sedilia* (seats for the priests officiating, cut into the south wall) became a common feature in the chancel; there is a fine set at PICKERING (North Yorkshire). Facing them on the opposite (north) wall was an Easter Sepulchre, the use of which reflected the theatrical style of service by then practised; a consecrated wafer was 'entombed' in it on Good Friday and 'raised' out of it again on Easter Sunday. Decorated fonts were often octagonal, and raised on a stepped platform.

Windows increased in size and their tracery became more and more elaborate. Assembled from intricately cut pieces of stone, their designs were initially geometric, drawn with compasses. Shortly before the end of the 13th century, the 'S' curve was adopted, opening the way to flowing or curvilinear tracery of the kind seen at BISHOPSTONE (Wiltshire). This decoration was also reflected in the carving of the font, or the ornamentation of chapel and chancel screens. This flamboyance was even more exaggerated in Scotland, as can be seen at HADDINGTON (Lothian). *Ballflower* (a three-petalled flower enclosing a small ball) and the four-leaf flower replaced dogtooth and nailhead as popular decoration on arches, windows and doorways.

Pillars are often taller than before, built to a variety of cross-sections – such as a diamond of clustered shafts. The decoration on capitals also changed in character during this period, becoming 'flattened out'. The emphasis was on the surface pattern rather than on three-dimensional ornament. The leaves are now more naturalistic – at CLAYPOLE (Lincolnshire) fronds of hawthorn and bryony and other hedgerow plants can be recognized. They are, however, carved in lower relief and seem 'pasted' on, quite unlike the deep-cut Early English style.

If there is roof vaulting, it can be structurally daring, but this is not obvious from below. The extra ribs which race up to the ridge or create star patterns are for decorative rather than structural purposes.

Effigies of knights and brasses from this period are quite common, while stained glass of the 14th century has rich colouring, as can be seen at STANFORD ON AVON (Northamptonshire). Porches become more common, and there is an increase in the number of spires – that on the bell tower at ASTBURY (Cheshire) is probably of this period. A timber tower and spire probably of about the same date can be seen at HIGH HALDEN (Kent).

A DECORATED WINDOW

OTHER CHURCHES
Ottery St Mary (Devon) is an intact Decorated church. Many churches, such as Molland (Devon), have carved Decorated capitals. Early geometrical tracery windows can be seen at Long Wittenham (Oxfordshire) and Chalton (Hampshire); Beeston (Norfolk) has fine flowing tracery while the windows at Leominster (Hereford and Worcester) have ballflowers added to the tracery. East-coast churches are often good places to look for features from this period: Pickworth (Lincolnshire) has a 14th-century Doom and other paintings. Great Bardfield and Stebbing (both in Essex) have fine stone screens with roods combined. Decorated sedilia can be seen at Cliffe (Kent) and many others. North Hinksey (Oxfordshire) is one of the many to echo the window tracery on its font. Chartham (Kent) has the very elaborate, starlike tracery typical of that county.

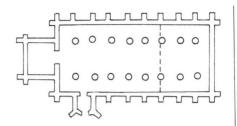

A PERPENDICULAR CHURCH PLAN

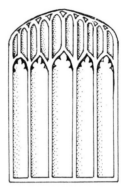

A PERPENDICULAR WINDOW

ELABORATE PERPENDICULAR SCREEN

GOTHIC: PERPENDICULAR

As the country recovered from the Black Death, abandoned manor lands became sheep runs. Feudalism was dying. People began to demand wages for their labour, and a new middle class was emerging. The Wars of the Roses enmeshed the whole country in turmoil for a century.

At this time a style of Gothic, not seen outside England, developed. Perpendicular had its beginnings soon after the Black Death, in Gloucester Cathedral, but it is in such buildings as King's College Chapel, Cambridge (1450s), and many country churches that it can be seen at its best. Some churches with fine Perpendicular features are in what were once rich 'wool' villages – a testimony to the vast wealth which a canny eye for trade could bring to small communities.

In time, the centres of trade in wool and cloth shifted westwards, leaving three main groups of Perpendicular wool churches: in East Anglia at FRESSINGFIELD and LAVENHAM (both in Suffolk) and SALL (Norfolk), for example; in the Cotswolds at such places as NORTHLEACH (Gloucestershire); and in the West Country at ASHTON (Devon) and many other places. But the new wealth was not restricted to these areas, and Perpendicular churches can also be found in the North – at TICKHILL (South Yorkshire) and KIRKBY MALHAM (North Yorkshire). GRESFORD (Clwyd), always a poor place, also has a fine Perpendicular church – perhaps because it held relics to attract the offerings of pilgrims.

About half of the 10,000 churches in Britain which are classed as architecturally important are 'Perpendicular', either in whole, as at HILLESDEN (Buckinghamshire), or in part, as at ISLE ABBOTS (Somerset).

ISLE ABBOTS has the tall and splendidly ornamented (and spireless) west tower which is often a signpost of this style. A number of characteristics mean that a Perpendicular church is immediately recognizable, including a splendid porch such as that at NORTHLEACH, a parapet hiding the roof, and a prominent row of clerestory windows as well as large windows elsewhere. Indeed some walls seem to be more glass than stone. Within, all is lofty, and spacious, too. The plan of the church is now rectangular, with aisles joining up to the transepts and often continuing as side chapels alongside the chancel.

The Victorian description 'Perpendicular' sums up the style. With its vertical runs of straight lines, it can be seen partly as a reaction against the sideways curvilinear fussiness of 'Decorated'. The pillars are lean and tall, and seem to flow in an unbroken line into the arch above, for the capitals are plainer and less prominent. Vertical lines dominate the patterns of the windows, fonts and other features. EDINGTON (Wiltshire) shows better than anywhere else the transition from Decorated to this new style: the large window has thin vertical mullions (strips, often of stone, dividing the window into lights) which either rise to the arch without a break, or diverge near the top to create panels between the vertical lines; strengthening is by horizontal transoms of either wood or stone.

While still 'pointed', the arch became flatter, and the arch of the doorway was often set within a square hood mould. The four-centred 'Tudor' arch became increasingly common in the 16th century.

Unless replenished with Victorian glass, today's Perpendicular churches are coolly lit, for the Reformation and Puritan movements vandalized them soon after completion. But a 15th- and 16th-century set of glass survives at FAIRFORD (Gloucestershire), which shows the original effect. Screens, too, were at their most elaborate, and often had strong local character, though few survive. ST MARGARET'S (Hereford and Worcester) has lacy carving typical of the area, and CULLOMPTON (Devon) has a fan-vaulted top. Rood lofts were widespread, used by the choir and musicians. Pulpits became prominent features (there is an early example at NORTHLEACH), and stalls, benches and *misericords* (a prop under tip-up choir seats, to ease standing during the long services) were often quaintly carved, as at BRENT KNOLL (Somerset) and FAIRFORD.

The most marvellous roofs ever were made during this period. There were various types. Stone fan vaulting is the glory of many chapels, but examples are found in country churches, such as in an aisle at CULLOMPTON and in many porches. Roofing was more often wooden, however, and highly decorated: this is the period of tie-beam roofs, wagon roofs and hammer-beam roofs, including the famous 'angel roofs' of East Anglia.

But when the Perpendicular was at its peak, there came the Reformation, with disastrous consequences for so much of the decoration of the previous centuries.

OTHER CHURCHES
Tall west towers are found in 'wool' areas: Shepton Mallet and Huish Episcopi are two well-known examples from Somerset, but towers can be found elsewhere, even in remote Cornwall, as at Morwenstow. Other famous almost-complete churches are at Thaxted (Essex), Ilminster (Somerset) and Long Melford (Suffolk). Addlethorpe (Lincolnshire), Ardleigh (Essex) and Launceston (Cornwall) have fine porches – the last of which is built of granite. North Leigh (Oxfordshire) has fine fan vaulting. Beautiful roofs of the period include the wagon roof at Watchet (Somerset) and the hammer-beam roof at Knapton (Norfolk).

◆

FROM SAXON TO GOTHIC

Although each architectural period has its own recognizable style, the country church on the whole changed more slowly. But change it did. Saxon and Norman churches had a similar feel to today's Russian or Greek Orthodox churches – they were simple in plan and dimly lit with few, narrow windows. Worship was impersonal, aided by slow, ponderous chants.

Candles or tapers did, however, reveal the presence of the *great rood*, usually painted above the chancel arch. The rood (meaning a cross) depicted Jesus suffering, with Mary and St John the Baptist to either side. A desecrated Saxon stone-carved rood remains at BREAMORE (Hampshire). The rood was not the only painted image in the early churches. The plastered nave walls sometimes had depictions of saints and religious scenes painted in ochre, and the Normans were also fond of patterned decoration as can be seen at COMPTON (Surrey). If the sanctuary ended with an apse, the wall might be painted with Christ in Majesty, as at COPFORD GREEN (Essex).

A 'wool brass' (c. 1525) in the Cotswold church at Northleach

The magnificent rood screen in the church of St Andrew, Cullompton

The church was virtually empty: a font stood near the main door, covered to prevent theft of its water for sorcery; there was a chest for valuables and there may have been rudimentary seating for the infirm around the walls. But there were no benches and no pulpit. The bare floor would probably have been scattered with rushes for warmth.

A Gothic church was generally larger than its Saxon and Norman predecessors. And it was brightly lit, for the aisle and clerestory windows were bigger. The rood was by now a painted, wooden construction, which stood on a rood beam stretching across the chancel arch. (Any rood figures we see today are replacements; the originals were destroyed at the Reformation or during the Commonwealth.) Below the beam was a rood screen, which in some areas of the country was elaborate and colourful – that at CULLOMPTON (Devon) has a 'vaulted' top; that at ASHTON (Devon) has painted panels.

The rood beam was often broadened into a rood loft, a platform reached by a staircase mined into the chancel arch pier, which might be used by musicians and a few singers. Examples remain at LLANFILO (Powys) and ST MARGARET'S (Hereford and Worcester).

A painted Doom or Last Judgement often took the place of the rood on the chancel arch; it was a terrifying depiction, designed to keep the populace in order as much as anything. The sin of sloth, for example, if not checked, scarce benefited the master. There might also be paintings of saints and biblical scenes on other walls.

To the east of the rood screen, whose central doors were opened only during the service, was the chancel. This was usually much larger than the Norman equivalent, and square-ended. There might be stalls to each side for priests, patron and squire. These stalls were sometimes highly decorated, such as those at SALL (Norfolk). Further into this priestly domain, sedilia were cut into the south wall for those officiating at the service. Alongside the altar was a *piscina* for ritual washing of the communion vessels. A splendid example is at ISLE ABBOTS (Somerset).

The medieval altar itself was a massive slab of stone cut with five consecration crosses, while behind it was either a decorative screen, called a *reredos*, which was made of carved, painted panels, or a wall painting. Above the altar was the great east window. In the north wall of the chancel, opposite the sedilia, was an Easter sepulchre, a recess in which the sacrament was placed during Holy Week.

Alongside the chancel, there was frequently a Lady Chapel commemorating Mary, Our Lady of Mercy, who might intercede to save sinners from Hell. The transepts and aisles usually had chantries or ended in chantry chapels; these contained altars and were endowed by families or craft guilds, and were where mass was said to secure the release of the souls of the donors from purgatory.

By the 15th century, there were pulpits of wood or stone, such as the example at NORTHLEACH (Gloucestershire) and benches for the congregation. The sermon had become an important part of the service.

While the chancel was the responsibility of the Church, the parishioners themselves paid for the upkeep of the rest of the building, and took pride in doing so. Unlike in Norman times, the medieval Church celebrated prominent parishioners, with their self-financed effigies in stone and wood, or with their images and names on carved slabs or brasses set into the floor.

The Church establishment used its power to regulate people's behaviour in a number of ways. In Geoffrey Chaucer's *The Canterbury Tales*, for example, written at the end of the 14th century, the character called the Summoner travelled from village to village picking up gossip of sins, which ranged from adultery to slander – many of which would merit heavy fines at the Archdeacon's court. This 'tax' was on top of the burden of tithes. The Church insisted on its ancient privileges, but the richer it grew, so what had once been gladly given became a source of resentment.

Growing self-confidence, grievance and international politics were about to combine in a cataclysmic upheaval, the Reformation, which swept away much of the contents of the 15th-century church.

<hr/>

FROM REFORMATION TO RESTORATION

In medieval times, the Church in Britain was Catholic, and was controlled by Rome. It was presided over by a rich and powerful clergy, even if the vicars who actually administered the parishes were poor. The Black Death and the following turmoil of the Wars of the Roses loosened feudal ties and a new 'middle class' grew to match the clergy. By the time the first of the Tudors took the throne in 1485, there was widespread resentment against the clergy, many of whom were not above diverting tithes into their own pockets or were too poorly educated to fulfil their duties.

In 1534 Henry VIII made himself Supreme Head of the Church in England. By 1539 he was actively closing down the monasteries and selling off their lands. The ransacked buildings fell into ruins, although often, as at UP HOLLAND (Lancashire), part of the building became the parish church. Henry's break with Rome was political rather than religious, however, for the Pope refused to sanction the annulment of his marriage to Catherine of Aragon. The Dissolution of the Monasteries came about partly because he needed money to balance the nation's books.

The stage was being set for a fierce struggle between Catholics and Protestants, and not just in Britain. Throughout Europe, Protestants – those who *protested*

Right *The nave at Staunton Harold, one of the few churches built during the Commonwealth*

against the corruption of the Catholic Church and its intolerance towards reformers such as Martin Luther – were fighting to establish a Church of their own with a congregation of participants rather than spectators, and with the services in their own language rather than Latin.

Major changes swept the village church, when in 1547 Henry was succeeded by the nine-year-old Edward VI whose 'protectors' were fervent Protestants. The old Latin services and ceremonies were abolished and replaced by simpler forms in English. The new liturgy tended to ignore the chancel, using the nave only, with the altar replaced by a communion table. Symbols and signs of the old religion including holy water, confessions, candles and incense were declared illegal. Chantries were wrecked, because they embodied the Catholic belief in purgatory, and their endowments seized. Roods were torn down and replaced by royal coats of arms, and the rood screens and lofts suffered by association. Wall paintings were whitewashed over, and the statues of saints, whom Catholics thought able to intercede with God, were defaced.

Edward died in 1553. His successor, Mary Tudor, was an ardent Catholic who reversed the Protestant reforms, brought back the Catholic bishops, restored the laws against heresy (which included professing Protestantism) and burned hundreds at the stake. Her bloody reign lasted only five years, but when it ended, many more people were fervently Protestant in reaction.

Elizabeth I, who succeeded Mary in 1558, took a middle course to resolve the situation, for not only did the Catholics have to be curbed, but so did the growing number of Puritans. These extreme English Protestants believed that the national Church established by Elizabeth was still in need of further 'purification'. Under the Elizabethan settlement, preachers were limited to four sermons a year, on the quarterly communion days, a licence being required for more, to counter the danger of dissenting propaganda. Elizabeth insisted on an oath of allegiance from the Church. Like her father, Henry VIII, she was excommunicated by Rome. *The Book of Common Prayer*, authorized once again in her reign, was to join with the English Bible as the bedrock for the Anglican Church which eventually developed.

The following reign, that of James I (1603–25), saw the Elizabethan Anglican settlement come of age. The Authorized Version of the Bible was first published under James in 1611. He also ordered a pulpit be placed in every church, which explains the number of 'Jacobean' examples to be seen. An untouched interior of the time, with fine woodcarving, still exists at CROSCOMBE (Somerset).

James I insisted on the Divine Right of Kings to rule, a notion at odds with the growing sense of democracy growing from Puritan ideals. Although there had been a movement away from Puritanism, events came to a head when the struggle between James' successor, Charles I, and Puritan parliamentarians developed into the Civil War. The King was beheaded and a Commonwealth established under

Oliver Cromwell. These years saw the destruction of any remaining 'superstitious images and inscriptions' in churches. A Parliamentary decree of 1641, for example, ordered the destruction of all stained-glass windows, for many still carried depictions of saints and the Holy Family.

During the Commonwealth, merriment was largely abolished. The church was by now empty of its ancient colour and glory, as well as of its hierarchy. The physical separation of priest and people was lessened: the pulpit was placed next to a nave wall, and the communicants took communion around a table set in the middle of the chancel (if it was still usable) – an arrangement which survives only in DEERHURST (Gloucestershire). Few churches were built during this period – STAUNTON HAROLD (Leicestershire) is a notable exception.

With the Restoration of the Monarchy, when Charles II came to the throne in 1660, the strict simplicity of the Puritans lost its grip on the national Church and the old Anglican spirit was restored. The altar was returned to the chancel end, although the pulpit remained in a prominent position in the nave. An Act of Uniformity of 1662 imposed on the clergy the Elizabethan prayer book still in use today.

THE RISE OF CLASSICISM

A new development in church design in the 17th century was the adoption of the classical architecture of the Continent. The Renaissance – 'rebirth' – was the revival of the spirit of ancient 'classical' Greece and Rome. It originated in Italy in the 15th century, but Britain was generally slow to adopt its ideas for building and the Gothic style continued sporadically here throughout the 17th century, in such churches as STAUNTON HAROLD (Leicestershire).

Classically inspired buildings are unmistakable. Among the hallmarks are the dome over the crossing and the *portico* (a porch like a temple front) with columns in one of the classical orders of architecture: Doric, Ionic, Corinthian, Tuscan or Composite. The exterior of such buildings can range from the exuberant, decorated with urns, swags of leaves or fruit, to the austerity and purity of some mid 18th-century buildings.

Classical motifs began to appear on buildings and monuments in England during the Reformation, in the 16th century – but only as decorative elements on otherwise traditional structures. In Henry VIII's reign, ideas were introduced mainly from France and were used in royal buildings and courtiers' homes, such as Old Somerset House in London. In country churches, classical motifs are restricted to the decoration of monuments, such as the Dormer tomb of 1552 at WING (Buckinghamshire).

A CLASSICAL WINDOW

A CLASSICAL MOULDING

In the 1560s and 1570s, classical ideas came mainly from Flanders and Holland, brought over the English Channel by Protestant refugees. There was a lack of real understanding of the system and forms being used, until the work of Inigo Jones (1573–1652), Britain's first 'architect'. (From this point, named individual architects appear in building history – the identity of most medieval masons is lost to us.)

Inigo Jones had visited Rome and studied classical ruins and more modern buildings, particularly those of the Venetian architect Andrea Palladio (1508–80), the author of *Quattro Libri dell' Architettura* (*Four Books of Architecture*), which were to have a profound influence on English architecture over the next three centuries. The influence of Palladio's ideas on Jones' work can be seen clearly in the Queen's House at Greenwich (1616–35). As well as royal buildings, Jones designed a church for the Duke of Bedford: St Paul's, Covent Garden (1630–1), with a portico of Tuscan columns.

During the Commonwealth, very few churches were built, but six years after the Restoration of the Monarchy, the Great Fire of London in 1666 provided Sir Christopher Wren with an opportunity to rebuild many of the City's churches, including St Paul's Cathedral, in a new style.

Although St Paul's is dominated by its vast (classical) dome, many of Wren's churches are characterized by their (unclassical) spires. Some of his churches have a nave and aisles, with transepts, but many are *auditory*, virtually square with galleries and laid out so that everyone could take part in the service and see what was going on. FARLEY (Wiltshire) adopts many of Wren's ideas and INGESTRE (Staffordshire) was almost certainly built to his design in 1676. The latter has 'Tuscan' compound piers and an ornate plasterwork ceiling.

Wren's churches and those of his contemporaries are mainly built in the Baroque style, which manipulates the pure forms of classical architecture to overwhelm the viewer emotionally. St Paul's Cathedral has an immense feeling of weight, and Thomas Archer's St Paul's, Deptford (1712–30), has the typical exaggeration of forms and dramatic use of light and shade. Country churches echoed the developments in London, and GAYHURST (Buckinghamshire) is a wholly English Baroque building of 1728, with contemporary furnishings. ABBOTTS ANN (Hampshire), built in 1716, and BLANDFORD FORUM (Dorset) of 1739 were both fairly typical of the style.

Scotland's church architecture developed in a slightly different direction; DURISDEER (Dumfries and Galloway) is an excellent example of this.

Palladio's influence on architecture is very important from about 1710 to about 1750. It is seen mainly in town houses and country villas, but one important church in the style is James Gibbs' St Martin-in-the-Fields in London (1721–6). In Palladian buildings, the pure classical forms are used again, without the exaggeration of the Baroque style.

Right *The classical orders of architecture*

OTHER CHURCHES

There were in general few new churches built during the Reformation, but Kilkhampton (Cornwall) of 1567, and Holcot (Bedfordshire) of 1590, are exceptions. Brooke (Leicestershire) is a rare example of a church that was rebuilt in the Elizabethan period. Low Ham (Somerset) was finished in 1669, and is still Perpendicular, but Berwick-upon-Tweed (Northumberland) of 1652 has a mixture of Gothic and classical features. Splendid Renaissance monuments can be seen in Lydiard Tregoze (Wiltshire). Willen (Buckinghamshire) of 1680 echoes Wren's ideas for the City of London churches. There are fine 18th-century churches at Tyberton (Hereford and Worcester), and Babington (Somerset). Nuneham Courtenay (Oxfordshire), Ayot St Lawrence (Hertfordshire), and Gunton (Norfolk) are classical 'temples', and Wilby (Norfolk) has a fine set of 17th-century church furniture.

DORIC

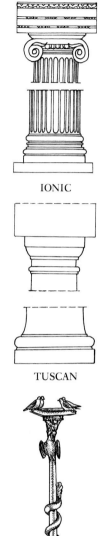

IONIC

CORINTHIAN

TUSCAN

COMPOSITE

CLASSICAL FONT

Ingestre – possibly the only country church built to Wren's design

Books on Renaissance and classical architecture were used for inspiration and reference. The interior of WEST WYCOMBE (Buckinghamshire), for example, is closely modelled on a 5th-century BC temple at Palmyra in Syria, which was featured in a book called *The Ruins of Palmyra*, published ten years earlier, in 1753. GREAT PACKINGTON (Warwickshire), built from 1789 to 1790, raided various books on Greek architecture for ideas. These are both examples of the neo-classical style of the late 18th century.

Although 'classical' buildings were erected all over Britain in the 18th century, Gothic did not die out, and by the middle of the century the Gothic Revival had begun. Gothic decorative forms were kept, but were supposedly 'improved' by using them according to the rules of classical architecture. One example was the 'Strawberry Hill Gothic', named after Horace Walpole's country house in Middlesex, built from 1748 onwards. SHOBDON (Hereford and Worcester) was rebuilt in 1753 and its interior is a delightful example of the style. Colour is often important: here simply white and blue are used to great effect.

◆

THE VICTORIANS

At the beginning of the 19th century, the Anglican village church was sleeping quietly, secure in its class divisions, rank being seen as part of God's provision. The squire dozed through the sermon in his box pew and the rector was himself frequently a hunting man. Alternatives were on offer not only from Catholics, but also from Nonconformists, Baptists and others of Puritan persuasion. An austere meeting place, Keach's Meeting House remains at Winslow in Buckinghamshire, complete with its original furniture. But although chapels were built in many villages, they brought an unwelcome hint of social strife and a strong parish might keep them out. Nonconformist chapels are more often found where the squires were less dominant.

Architecture, however, did not stand still. In the 1820s the classical taste spawned even purer 'Greek Revival' churches, of which GREAT PACKINGTON (Warwickshire), finished in 1790, had been a precursor. But as the century progressed, two main camps (both revivalist) emerged – classical and Gothic. Town halls, railway stations and churches were all affected by these movements.

The Church, which was seen as extremely corrupt, was reformed in the 1830s; tithes were abolished, as were taxes levied for church-building. Influential ecclesiological societies wished for a return to the piety and ritual of the medieval Church. Gothic, or specifically 14th-century Decorated architecture, was seen as the 'correct' style to promote this. New churches were built in variations of the Decorated style. They were built mainly in the booming towns and cities

*Late medieval bench ends at Launcells,
a church overlooked by Victorian
restorers*

The pulpit and reading desk are combined at St Mary's, Whitby

spawned by the Industrial Revolution, but BRADFIELD (Berkshire), largely rebuilt then, is a village example. However, correctness did not always suppress originality. A strong-minded architect could impose his own whims: BRAMPTON (Cumbria), reviled as a 'warehouse', owed little to the ecclesiologists' correct style, while the rector wittily put elephants' heads in the roof of WICKHAM (Berkshire)!

Old churches were also 'restored' in an attempt to re-create 'correct' Gothic. This often meant that the building was stripped of all except the memorials to the dead. The original plaster, and the hidden wall paintings (that is, those plastered over during the Reformation or Commonwealth), were stripped off to lay the stone bare. Old wooden pews and box pews were thrown out, or cut down. Old tiles and stone flags were torn from the floors. In their place were put low-backed, pitch-pine pews and shiny new tiles of garish colour and design. This Victorian attempt to re-create Gothic religious feeling often destroyed what was truly Gothic.

The western gallery, which had been installed to replace the rood loft, and on which the choir and orchestra (or organ) had been placed in Georgian times, was torn down. Singers clad in surplices now occupied part of the chancel in stalls which imitated the choir stalls of abbeys. The altar was now back in place under the east window at the end of the chancel, which was often rebuilt and enlarged. The organ was often replaced by one near the choir in the chancel, but it was usually so much larger that it dwarfed its surroundings.

The insensitivity of the zealous Victorian restorers can be seen in such specific anomalies as the addition of a 'Gothic' font to the Baroque splendour of GREAT WITLEY (Hereford and Worcester). More generally the Victorians spoiled their churches by their use of 'foreign' materials such as slates from Wales and polished marbles from Italy in the down-the-lane country churches built of local materials. But the heavy hand cannot quite kill the interest – LITTLE MAPLESTEAD (Essex) is still well worth a visit as a round-naved church of Crusader origin, despite the addition of a vestry, south porch, transepts, new window tracery, new roofs and the removal of all the external plaster. Happily, there had been some sensitive 'restorations', such as the Perpendicular HILLESDEN (Buckinghamshire) and the Norman DALMENY (Lothian). Some people did become concerned when restorations bordered on mutilation. The 'skinning alive' of BURFORD (Oxfordshire) sparked off an 'antiscrape' movement which led to the foundation in 1877 of the Society for the Protection of Ancient Buildings, our first amenity society. And indeed, in time, some churches positively benefited from such things as well-designed fonts, lecterns, and really fine glass windows by William Morris and Sir Edward Burne-Jones (although much Victorian glass tends to be garish).

Some churches escaped entirely, and among the churches the Victorians forgot are BLANDFORD FORUM (Dorset), which houses Georgian furnishings all of one

OTHER CHURCHES

There are fine Victorian interiors at Leiston (Suffolk) and Kingston (Dorset). St Martin's, Scarborough (North Yorkshire), has a fine 'Pre-Raphaelite' pulpit – an example of the imaginative furniture of the 19th century. The brass eagle lecterns at Bibury (Gloucestershire) and that of Tarrant Hinton (Dorset) are others. Victorian memorials such as that in Hafod (Dyfed) can be moving. Complete Victorian churches of special interest include Sausthorpe (Lincolnshire), which is almost entirely built of white brick. Holy Trinity Church at Chapel Stile, Great Langdale (Cumbria), was built in the local green slate to cater for a rapidly increasing population. Martindale (Cumbria) was built in around 1882, but in the Early English style. Brockhampton-by-Ross (Hereford and Worcester), designed in 1901, has been called 'a temple to the Arts and Crafts Movement' because of its exquisite carvings, tapestries and stained glass. Seaham (County Durham) is a Saxon and 13th-century church, tastefully restored in about 1913, even to the extent of leaving the box pews intact.

date, WHITBY (North Yorkshire), WARHAM ST MARY (Norfolk), INGLESHAM (Wiltshire), LAUNCELLS (Cornwall) and – perhaps most charming of all – MINSTEAD (Hampshire), all of which contain a medley of different ages.

TOWERS, SPIRES AND ROOFS

Towers are a powerful visible symbol of the importance of the church. They were often a feature in Saxon and especially Norman days, when they were often capped with a low pyramid as seen at PENMON (Gwynedd). Many Norman towers had to be replaced later, because they were too ambitious and collapsed. Gothic towers were also sometimes built at the west end of the nave. These created the familiar 'two steps down' (tower-nave-chancel) profile of country churches. Towers reached their prime in the Perpendicular period, ornately decorated with pinnacles, lacelike parapets ('battlements') and niches for statues.

Tall spires are the crowning feature of many churches. They were added in the Early English period, and in the Decorated, but Perpendicular towers were impressive enough without. The earliest lead-covered wooden spire is at LONG SUTTON (Lincolnshire), and dates from the 14th century. Many early spires are, however, shingled with split (not cut) oak 'tiles', which have to be replaced every 70 years or so. GREAT BOOKHAM (Surrey) is one example.

Round spires were difficult to build and clad, especially in stone. An octagonal spire is normal, but set on a square tower it leaves gaps at each corner which look ugly and also collect rain and snow. One solution was to add a small pinnacle at each corner, as at LONG SUTTON. BARNACK (Cambridgeshire) has an early 13th-century spire, set on a pinnacled octagonal base. Another solution was the *broach spire* (the triangular gaps were covered by masonry sloping up from the tower corner to the side of the spire). Sometimes the join between tower and spire might be hidden behind a parapet such as the buttressed example at YAXLEY (Cambridgeshire). The broach spire, in particular, was often decorated with spire lights for ventilation and even with statues. The weather vane is a common sight at the top of a church spire – the popular image is a cock (recalling St Peter who denied Christ three times before cockcrow) although many are heraldic.

Towers, of course, carry clocks. Dials did not appear until the 17th century on village church towers; until then the clock simply struck the quarters, sometimes with small mechanical figures or jacks. The tower had the additional job of housing the bells, one of which served as the curfew bell – a bell which was for many centuries rung each evening as warning that the hut fires should be extinguished and the villagers stay within doors until the next morning. Failing a tower, a *bellcote* (usually a small arch) was necessary.

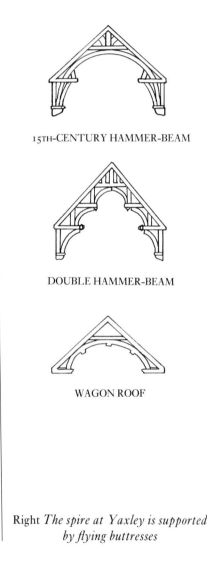

15TH-CENTURY HAMMER-BEAM

DOUBLE HAMMER-BEAM

WAGON ROOF

Right *The spire at Yaxley is supported by flying buttresses*

The roofs of early country churches can be of outstanding workmanship. Most early ones are Gothic, but a Norman roof of matched adze-trimmed oak boughs has been found hidden behind a later ceiling in the chancel of STANFORD ON AVON (Northamptonshire). Some of the finest roofs which exist today date from the Perpendicular period. One development from the early tie-beam roof, which has a cross-strut to span the distance and prevent the walls being pushed out, was the hammer-beam, a way of spanning a nave wider than available timbers could reach. The ornately decorated timbers sometimes end with carved angels such as at MILDENHALL (Suffolk). When painted, these roofs are spectacular. In another development, seen at BRENT KNOLL (Somerset), for example, cambered beams support decorated panels. Curved beams were often boarded to create a boat-like keel roof or a more rounded wagon roof, typically in the West Country. When lead became used instead of tiling in Perpendicular and later times, the pitch flattened to prevent the lead 'creeping'.

Perpendicular masonry matched the splendour of these timber roofs with fan vaulting. Although a feature of great chapels such as King's College, Cambridge, this form of vaulting is occasionally found in aisles and chapels in country churches, as at CULLOMPTON (Devon) – a church which also boasts a fine wagon roof – and in porches.

* * *

WALL PAINTINGS AND WINDOWS

We see the inside of today's medieval church as a bleached skeleton. The Reformation stripped it of its intense colour when an Order of the King's Council of 1547 urged the 'obliteration and destruction of popish and superstitious images so that the memory of them shall not remain in churches'.

Before that, colour ran across the rood screen and the chantry screens, glowed from the wall paintings and beamed through the stained-glass windows. It is likely that the font, the pillar capitals and other carved decoration were also painted. Today, perhaps only the painted wooden roof remains, as it does in many Perpendicular churches.

Some colour has been replaced – many windows now carry Victorian or later glass and bright floor tiles, but, apart from those 2000 or so churches in which paintings or fragments of them have been discovered under the plaster, the walls remain bare except for the heraldic Georgian funeral *hatchments* (diamond-shaped painted boards) and other memorials. From those paintings which do remain, we can attempt to reconstruct the splendour that once existed.

The Normans sometimes patterned whole walls: at COMPTON (Surrey) traces remain of a sophisticated optical illusion – a 'staircase' which changes from rising

OTHER CHURCHES

There is a stone spire of 1240 at Witney (Oxfordshire). East Meon (Hampshire) and Braunton (Devon) have lead spires, and thin leaded 'needle' spires (spirelets) can be seen in Hertfordshire and neighbouring counties, as at Flamstead and Little Hadham. Broach spires are fairly common, such as those at Etton (Northamptonshire) and Holme (Nottinghamshire). Louth (Lincolnshire) has a fine parapet spire. A 15th-century clock jack striking the bell can be seen at Southwold (Suffolk); an early one-handed clock face is at Coningsby (Lincolnshire). Many clock faces, as at Long Stratton (Norfolk), were added in the 18th century.

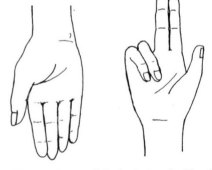

*Decorative symbols depicting the Hand of God in judgement (*left*) and in blessing (*right*)*

The upper part of the Last Judgement window at the west end of St Mary's, Fairford

43

to descending at the blink of an eye, and perhaps represents the slippery path to salvation. However, a formalized set of paintings became usual and education-ally necessary, for before the Reformation both Bible and liturgy were in Latin, which few could understand. The faithful could learn from the paintings, and be fearful at the scenes shown.

With the rood on the rood beam, the chancel arch above often carried a Doom, a vivid depiction of the Last Judgement. YAXLEY (Cambridgeshire) has some frag-ments of late 15th-century date. The other walls might carry portraits of saints, especially St Michael and St Christopher – the latter facing the main door, so that he could be easily seen by wayfarers. As the patron saint of travellers he could (for the price of a prayer) intercede if calamity struck on the journey. PICKER-ING (North Yorkshire) has a varied number of scenes from the lives of saints and others, painted in the 15th century. The curved apse of the sanctuary was also painted; few apses remain, but that at COPFORD GREEN (Essex) still has its Christ in Majesty above the altar, as well as scenes over the other walls. These all date from the 12th century.

Some ceilings were decorated after the Reformation – scenes from the Creation were painted on the ceiling of STAUNTON HAROLD (Leicestershire) in the 17th century.

Very little early glass survived the Reformation or the Commonwealth. Although 12th-century glass can be seen at RIVENHALL (Essex), it was brought from abroad. Coloured glass was probably first seen in country churches in the 13th century, as simple two-dimensional images on small *quarries* (panes) held between thick lead 'cames'. The earliest of this coloured glass was uneven 'pot' glass, of one deep colour throughout. Later, coloured sheets were flashed or annealed on to quarries of plain glass. In time the depiction of shading improved. Clear glass ornamented in muted colours with delicate patterns became popular, giving a clearer light within the church than was possible if all windows were heavily coloured. Heraldry was always popular, as was the Jesse window, tracing Christ's family tree from the 'root of Jesse'. Examples are at WESTWELL (Kent) and DORCHESTER (Oxfordshire), which also has wonderful 12th-century glass in the round windows behind the sedilia.

In Perpendicular churches, figures filled the panelling of the windows: 'lean windows filled with fat saints', as Horace Walpole described them. Rare surviving examples show us what we have lost. A marvellous complete set dating from 1500 remains at FAIRFORD (Gloucestershire); and a window at STANFORD ON AVON (Northamptonshire) survived forgotten in a chest in a nearby mansion. There is an interesting 15th-century east window at EAST HARLING (Norfolk), which includes figures of those responsible for rebuilding this Perpendicular church; it too was discovered hidden in the local manor house.

It is sad that so little of this glory remains. Colour did return to glass, more

Right Decorative symbols of the Holy Trinity included the Trefoil and the Three Fishes

OTHER CHURCHES
Many churches have slight traces of wall paintings, even if only a short span of decorative motif on a window arch. Baunton (Gloucestershire), Ridge (Hertfordshire) and Wedmore (Somerset) each have a St Christopher; South Leigh (Oxfordshire) and Bartlow (Cambridgeshire) contain a St Michael, and Wenhaston (Suffolk) a Doom. Glass was sometimes purloined for use in local houses at the Reformation – and vice versa afterwards. Yarnton (Oxfordshire) has a fragment with a bird and the inscription 'who blamyth this ale', which has clearly been taken from an inn! A complete 14th-century window can be seen at Selling (Kent), and saints at Heydour (Lincolnshire) and Kempey (Hereford and Worcester) are of roughly the same date. East Brent (Somerset) has a window depicting the Passion, from the 15th century. Some modern glass, such as that of Abinger (Surrey), is a delight. Burghclere (Berkshire) has a series of murals painted by Stanley Spencer in 1928–9 in memory of those killed in World War I, and Berwick (East Sussex) is a 12th-century church that has a series of murals painted by members of the Bloomsbury Group in the 1940s.

TREFOIL   THREE FISHES

delicately than before, in the early 17th century, being enamelled rather than in the older annealed tradition. Daylight was welcomed for its own sake in Georgian days and colour was restrained. Ponderous colouring returned in Victorian days (the Great Exhibition of 1851 fostered interest in stained glass), although some workshops such as that of William Morris produced windows of rare beauty, such as to be seen at BRAMPTON (Cumbria).

IN MEMORIAM

Clerics had been buried inside churches in Saxon times, and later other important people were too. It is probable, however, that the early coffin lids of 12th- and 13th-century date which are often seen inside a church have been brought in from the churchyard at some time. By the 13th century, rectangular tomb chests with the body usually buried below were common in cathedrals and abbeys. They commemorated the privileged, either state or church, whose carved effigy rested on top. The sides usually carried heraldic shields and other devices. During the 13th century, tombs with effigies of knights began to appear in country churches, carved in wood or stone. More of the latter survive of course. Figures are usually shown lying as if asleep, although a 13th-century example at DORCHESTER (Oxfordshire) draws his sword in a spirited fashion.

Apart from the interest of heraldic displays, these effigies show arms and armour in some detail and the tombs in some churches give an illustration of the changes in fashions which took place down the centuries: BOTTESFORD (Leicestershire) has one such series of tombs from the 13th to 17th centuries. Originally, the figures would have been painted.

The faces also become more personal and (presumably) lifelike from the 14th century. Only a few show the stark, true face of death. One tomb of 1475 at EWELME (Oxfordshire) has the skeleton lying below the customary sleeping figure. This, like many of the grander effigy tombs, has an elaborate canopy.

By the early 17th century, many of the figures are lolling on one elbow. By now, effigies were often in alabaster, quarried in Derbyshire and elsewhere – it was soft when first cut but hardened and could be polished and painted. These later monuments usually keep their colouring.

In the 14th century, double, husband-and-wife tombs became popular. Sometimes the wife lying alongside her husband has her right hand held in, or touching, his hand. This is not as romantic as it might seem, but denoted that she was heiress in her own right. At BRENT KNOLL (Somerset), a mid 17th-century monument shows a man accompanied by two wives, who died some years apart and are in very different headgear.

45

Exquisite carving on the 1563
monument to the second Earl of Rutland
at Bottesford

From around the middle of the 15th century on, the figures might be accompanied by small 'weepers' – depictions either of angels or of their own children. The monument to Sir Edward Lewis and his wife Anne, of 1630 at EDINGTON (Wiltshire), is just one example. Specific imagery allows the viewer to 'read' these tombs. If children are shown holding skulls, for example, it means that they had died before their father, while a half-sized or smaller effigy of an adult signified an heir who had died before his father.

Monuments of the early 17th century could be of great size and lavishly coloured. In the 18th century black or white marble and other exotic stone replaced alabaster, and the huge edifices often dwarfed the church. It was at this time, the period from around 1680 to 1760 when classicism was at its height, that many effigies were depicted in Roman dress, such as in a monument of 1686 at BOTTESFORD. They are often relaxed but accurate portraits. There is a splendid 18th-century example in GREAT WITLEY (Hereford and Worcester).

From the late 13th century on, and notably in the Decorated period, brasses began to be set in 'ledger' stones marking burials in the floor of the church. Just as effigies show changes in fashion, these brasses show the evolution of armour. In time they began to show the merchant classes rather than knights, as at BURFORD (Oxfordshire). Many brasses were, sadly, sold or destroyed during the Reformation and by the Puritans.

The Reformation had called a halt to the use of abbeys for the burial of grand personages, and in time floor space began to run out in other churches (the diarist John Evelyn in 1682 deplored the 'unhygienic' custom of floor burial). Where burial space remained, wall memorials became more common. Many were brasses; others carved in relief. An early one of 1492 in the north aisle of YOULGREAVE (Derbyshire) shows man, wife – and 17 children. Later these became simpler – a depiction of an urn perhaps, or simply an inscription of some kind. It became normal for these memorials to record the virtues of the departed.

Typical of Georgian times was the habit of fixing hatchments (painted with the coat of arms of the deceased) to the walls. There are 17 in STANFORD ON AVON (Northamptonshire). The colour of the background could denote the marital status of the deceased.

OTHER EFFIGIES

Wooden knightly effigies can be seen at Sparsholt (Oxfordshire) and Barnborough (South Yorkshire). Conisbrough (South Yorkshire) has an early tomb chest. There are pre-Reformation effigies at Feniton (Devon) – one with an image of a corpse. There is a Tudor one at Great Brington (Northamptonshire); 17th-century examples at Gawsworth (Cheshire) and Snarford (Lincolnshire), and some from the 18th century at Shute (Devon), Yarnton (Oxfordshire) and Strensham (Hereford and Worcester). The oldest brass of a knight is at Stoke d'Abernon (Surrey) of 1277; brasses depicting priests are seen in many places, as at Broadwater (West Sussex).

GOD'S ACRE

The church we see today is not always as old as its churchyard. Our word church is derived from an old word *ciric* (pronounced 'chirrich') which referred to holy ground or churchyard – a place of Christian burial. Circular or oval churchyards such as at ESCOMB (County Durham) seem to be linked with the old Celtic Church. Churchyards became roughly rectangular in Saxon times, when it became customary to consecrate an area of roughly one acre. The site chosen for a preaching-ground, and later for a churchyard, might be one of pre-Christian significance. BRENTOR (Devon) is on top of a hill, within an Iron Age fortification, and like many churches on old hilltop sites, it is dedicated to St Michael. It has been claimed that prehistoric religious sites on hills were associated with one particular god, and that when the Christians took over these sites, St Michael assumed some of the aspects of that pagan god. Other churchyards contain prehistoric standing stones, carved with crosses to adapt them to Christianity. There are examples of this in some Cornish churchyards.

Some Dark Age memorials echo fading Roman Christianity, with a scratched cross, but there were also well-carved crosses, which might have been preaching crosses, marking the venue for the minster priests, before a church was built on the site. Being carved with the rood, many were destroyed in the Reformation, but pieces may remain, as can be seen at LASTINGHAM (North Yorkshire). They sometimes carry runes, an alphabet used by Scandinavian (and sometimes Anglo-Saxon) peoples.

Almost all medieval churchyard crosses were destroyed in the Reformation and by the Puritans, and perhaps only the stump remains. There is, however, a complete example at DORCHESTER (Oxfordshire). They may have been erected to commemorate those buried in the churchyard, for individual gravestones did not appear until the 17th century. Numerous burials on rocky soil created problems and many churches had a charnel house, as at CAREW CHERITON (Dyfed), to store bones and so make space for later burials.

Memorials of stone last, and can be quite finely lettered, probably the work of a local craftsman. Those of marble and granite are quite recent – before Victorian days they were always made of local stone; but there are some from the 19th century at ABBOTTS ANN (Hampshire) in cast iron.

Chest tombs usually date from Georgian times; as is the case within the church, the body is buried not in the chest, but below. They sometimes took on other functions: for example, one in the churchyard at EDINGTON (Wiltshire) is known as the dole stone – here the free bread was doled out to the poor. And there was some local variety: the Cotswolds are notable for their 'bale' tombs, carved to represent a bale of wool, or even a corpse wrapped in one, as is to be seen at BURFORD (Oxfordshire) – for a time it was a legal requirement to be buried in a woollen shroud, a policy aimed at helping the English wool industry.

An important feature of many churchyards is the entrance gate, or lych gate (lych being an old word for corpse). Here the coffin rested to await the priest. The gate was often roofed to keep the party dry, and could be quite elaborate. There is a stone example at ASTBURY (Cheshire).

Social rank and money dictated where a person was buried in the church or

FUNERAL HATCHMENT

MEMORIAL TOMB BRASS

Right *The churchyard at Minstead, where Sir Arthur Conan Doyle is also buried*

churchyard and an epigram records this:

> *Here I lie at the chapel door,*
> *Here I lie because I'm poor,*
> *The further in the more you'll pay,*
> *Here I lie as warm as they. . . .*

The yew tree is associated with the churchyard and an old yew can be seen at BREAMORE (Hampshire) and many other places. According to tradition, the evergreen boughs of a yew sheltered the first Christian missionaries to come to Britain, and thereafter the trees were planted as a symbol of faith and immortality, being evergreen and long-lived. Rowan trees also occur regularly in churchyards, to ward off evil. But the association between these particular trees and churchyards may have come from pre-Roman, Celtic times. It seems to have been common practice for the early missionaries to take over pagan usages and sites rather than let them remain as rivals.

SOUNDS OF PRAISE

Although there are church bells in Wales and Scotland, the ripple of bells is an English sound – more than 5000 churches in England have peals of five or more bells. At least 3000 of these bells are medieval. Until the Reformation they were often dedicated to saints, but afterwards mottoes or donors' or makers' names were inscribed on them. Many of the bells in use, however, have been recast, perhaps because they were cracked, or to retune them to modern ears. STOW (Lincolnshire) is one of the few churches to keep its primitive tuning. Old bells are sometimes to be found displayed on the floor of tower or nave, as in BURFORD (Oxfordshire).

Church bells traditionally rang the morning awakening and the dusk curfew (which some churches continued to do up to the 19th century) and were used as alarms. They tolled at burials, rang gaily at weddings, and often marked the anniversary of the monarch's accession. At BRENTOR (Devon) they even rang out on Guy Fawkes Day for many years.

Before the 14th century they were chimed simply by pulling the rope to swing the bell so that the clapper struck, but mountings evolved so the bell could be swung right over. For a peal, each bell has to be swung to mouth-up position, where it hesitates before continuing with a marvellous clanging downward swing which carries it round, nearly to the top again.

By 1400 most churches had three bells, and their housing was partly the reason for the splendid west towers built at that time. As the number of bells grew,

OTHER CHURCHES
Knowlton (Dorset) is built within the banks of a New Stone Age henge, over 4000 years older; Rudston (Humberside) has a gigantic standing stone in the churchyard. There are fine Dark Age crosses at Bewcastle and Gosforth (both in Cumbria), and complete 15th-century churchyard crosses at Ampney Crucis (Gloucestershire) and Somerby (Lincolnshire). There are finely carved headstones at Cavendish (Suffolk) and Bladon (Oxfordshire), and a medieval lych gate at Anstey (Hertfordshire).

*The 17th-century organ loft at
Staunton Harold in Leicestershire*

'change ringing' became popular. Ringing the changes, with each bell passing in turn 'through' its companions, can be a long and arduous process; a thirsty one too – many pubs are called the Six Bells, and a few churches still keep their ringers' traditional giant beer mugs.

Elaborate timbering such as that seen at HIGH HALDEN (Kent) is needed within the tower to hold the bells, whose swings impose a great structural strain. The bells at WESTWELL (Kent) can no longer be rung, because the timbers are too weak. The bell tower at WEST WALTON (Norfolk) is quite far from the church, perhaps on firmer ground. Many churches never acquired a bell tower but have a more modest bellcote – such as the 13th-century one at INGLESHAM (Wiltshire).

Although sounds of praise have also echoed within the church since early times, the exact form of the medieval service is unclear. Plainsong – an intoned melody reflecting the rhythm of the words – was chanted and there was a choir and small orchestra on the rood loft. Later a small organ might be placed on the rood loft (giving the origin of the term 'organ loft'). Organs appear in many medieval churchwardens' accounts – at first some were small enough to be portable.

The zealots of the Commonwealth frowned on music, as they did on much use of bells, and a Puritan ordinance of 1644 made organs 'illegal in the worship of God'. The organ at STANFORD ON AVON (Northamptonshire) is one of the rare survivals from pre-Restoration times – and probably came from the Chapel Royal of Charles I in Whitehall, London.

In the years following the Restoration of the Monarchy in 1660, tuneful worship again became appreciated. Organs were again built and with cases that were fashionably decorated to suit the taste of the age. The organ at GREAT PACKINGTON (Warwickshire) is thought to have been designed by Handel.

The rood loft having usually been removed in Reformation and Puritan days, a new gallery was often built at the west end of the nave for the singers, the orchestra and for the organ if there was one, as seen at STANFORD ON AVON and at BLANDFORD FORUM (Dorset). A local orchestra was a feature of many a Georgian church, and some churches still keep their old instruments.

With the onset of Victorian High Church ambitions, however, the western gallery was often taken down, and the organ placed as near to the chancel as possible. In the chancel (which was often enlarged) the Victorians placed a choir dressed in surplices and seated in choir stalls.

Many Victorian organs were large and expensive – that at WICKHAM (Berkshire) cost £1000 in 1842. Their sheer size makes them intrusive in a medieval church, and even later churches find them difficult to fit – as can be seen at ABBOTTS ANN (Hampshire). Poorer parishes in Victorian times sometimes made do with barrel organs.

The oldest village bell may be that at Caversfield (Oxfordshire) which was made in 1207; it was not cast, but turned on a lathe in the ancient manner. Other medieval bells can be seen at Bartlow (Cambridgeshire) and Margaretting (Essex). The bell tower at Terrington (Norfolk) is separate from its church, while at East Bergholt (Suffolk) the bells are rung in a frame at ground level. Only one pre-Reformation organ remains, at Old Radnor (Powys), dating from early in the reign of Henry VIII; a pre-Restoration organ can be seen at Old Bilton (Warwickshire). Georgian instruments can also be seen, such as the clarionet at Old Alresford (Hampshire) and a pitch pipe at Easby (North Yorkshire). There is a barrel organ at Bresington (Norfolk) – and one at Avington (Hampshire) is still in use.

CHURCH AND COMMUNITY

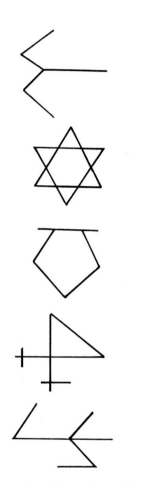

Examples of 'mason's marks'

The medieval church was the proper focus of extreme emotions for all. It provided not only powerful rebuke (the horror of Hell could be seen at first hand, spelled out in wall paintings) but also the ecstasy of hope brought by Holy Communion. It celebrated inevitable times of great joy and sadness – of baptism, marriage and death – for one and all, uniting all ranks of life in the village. But in past centuries it also acted as the village hall, a storehouse, and a refuge in emergencies.

Some echoes of this past reappear in unexpected ways in our language and culture. Before seating came into general use in churches, there was perhaps only a ledge for the infirm (who were still required to attend services) around the walls, as at PATRINGTON (Humberside). This is probably the origin of the expression 'going to the wall'.

The church may well have housed refugees from plague or other disasters, and it often acted as a refuge in times of flood, as it was often on the highest ground in the area. Anxious refugees and villagers scratched 'graffiti' on the walls of some churches. There is a Viking longboat at STOW (Lincolnshire), and ASH-WELL (Hertfordshire) has a varied collection of graffiti, including poignant references to the plague.

The church was not only a place of asylum for miscreants (or supposed wrong-doers) in a panic and seeking sanctuary – a sanctuary ring to knock for admittance can be seen at FELMERSHAM (Bedfordshire) – but also in times of strife. The 'peel' churches of the North, with their castle-like towers, were strongholds against cattle raiders. Similarly, the tower at ASTBURY (Cheshire) housed the women when Welsh cattle raiders swept into the parish. KIRKBY MALHAM (North Yorkshire) has an 'invasion beam' to secure the door. During the Civil War, many churches were besieged – the holes in the door of HILLESDEN (Buckinghamshire) were made by Roundhead bullets.

Scratched features to look for within the church are *mason's marks*, by which the craftsmen identified their work; they are found especially in later Norman and Gothic churches, such as COMPTON (Surrey), while there is a good set of the more elaborate *consecration crosses* at EDINGTON (Wiltshire). These marked the 24 places, 12 inside and 12 outside, where the bishop anointed a church at its consecration. In the days before clocks, many churches had a *sundial* – there is a good Saxon example at ESCOMB (County Durham) – or a simpler *scratch dial* to indicate the times of services.

Evidence can also be found of anchorites' cells, where a penitent was walled up, usually for life. At COMPTON, a small window in the north wall of the chancel allowed the anchorite to see the service. The cell itself is no longer there.

Victorian zeal has distanced the church of old. Nobody today, for example, would take a dog into a church, but it was once quite usual. Indeed, in CLYNNOG-

A funerary banner at Staunton Harold in Leicestershire

OTHER CHURCHES

Clifton Hampden (Oxfordshire) has old wall seats; at Hunstanton and Snettisham (both in Norfolk) they are around pillars. Cley (Norfolk) is one of the many with fine sundials on the porch; Barfreston (Kent) has many scratch dials. At Shere (Surrey), the vague outline of the anchoress's cell can be seen on the outside of the north wall of the chancel. Grooves worn by dog chains are seen on shepherds' pews at Stanton (Gloucestershire). Civil War bullets can be seen in the door at West Hoathly (West Sussex), while some of the wall stones have been used as arrow whets (sharpening stones) at Eccleshall (Staffordshire). Leominster (Hereford and Worcester) stores a ducking stool, and Chacely (Gloucestershire) the village stocks, while Mendlesham (Suffolk) still keeps 15th- and 17th-century armour in a room over the porch.

FAWR (Gwynedd) there are iron dog tongs to control the shepherds' irritable animals. In fact, the 'Laudian' communion rails, which take their name from Archbishop Laud who introduced them in 1634, were partly to stop dogs from fouling the most sacred part of the church.

The church was a useful village storehouse. The weapons and armour of the local militia might be kept in it together with stocks and other instruments of punishment. Great fire hooks to tear the thatch from a burning cottage still hang in EATON BRAY (Bedfordshire). In early times, 'church ales' – feasts and dancing – were held in the empty nave. They were initiated by Pope Gregory VII (1073–85) to replace pagan festivals of sacrifice and feast, but when the church began to fill with benches and other furniture they were often held in the porch.

Some church porches (usually on the south side as the north doors were generally used for Palm Sunday and other ceremonial processions) are very elaborate constructions, whether of stone such as at NORTHLEACH (Gloucestershire) and FRESSINGFIELD (Suffolk) or of wood as at HIGH HALDEN (Kent). The upper room of two-storeyed porches, such as at NORTHLEACH and FRESSINGFIELD, could serve as a bedroom for the priest taking early service, or as an extra schoolroom. The porch itself often served as a village school.

Those who broke vows did penance in the porch, swathed in a white wrap, and part of the baptismal rites took place here as did the first part of the marriage service. Chaucer's Wife of Bath in *The Canterbury Tales* had five husbands 'at chirche dore'. Parish meetings and other village business were conducted here, including disputes over animals (which might be pounded in the churchyard to await the result). The church porch is still a place for local notices.

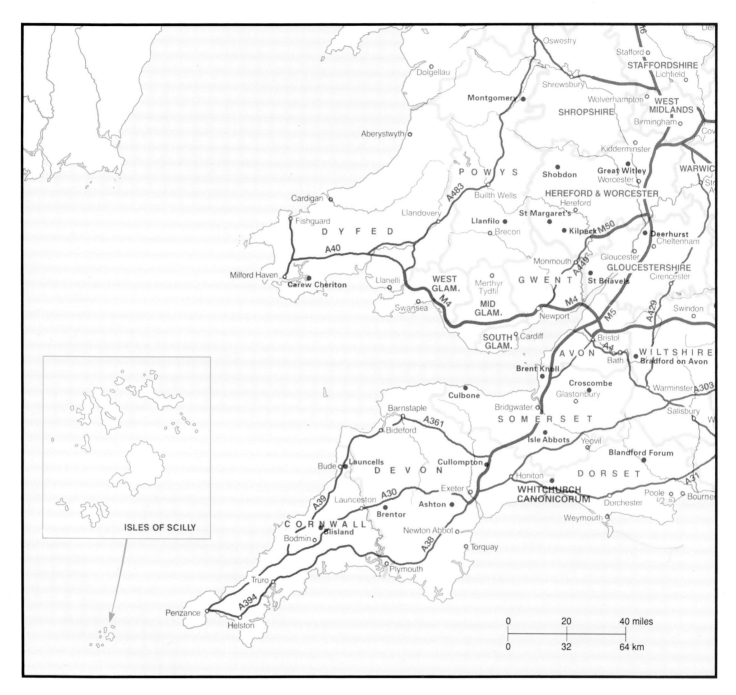

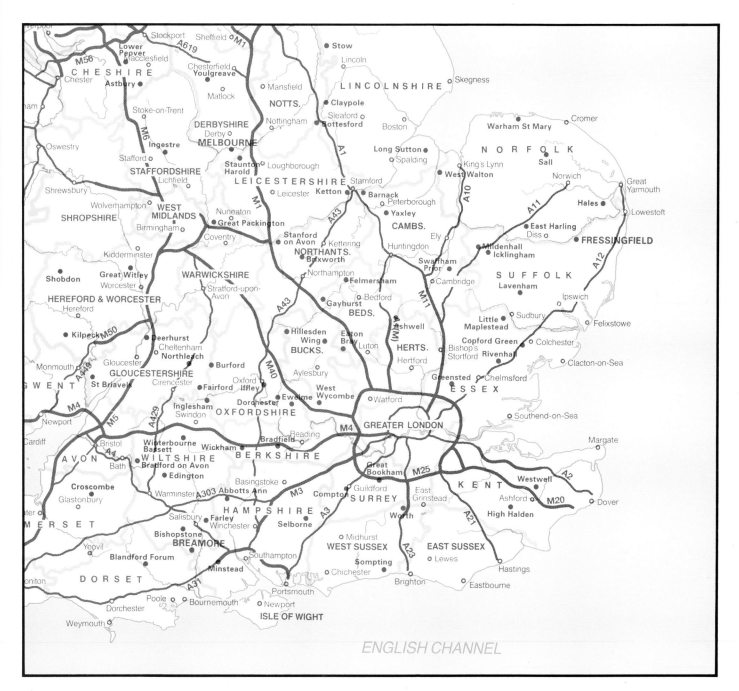

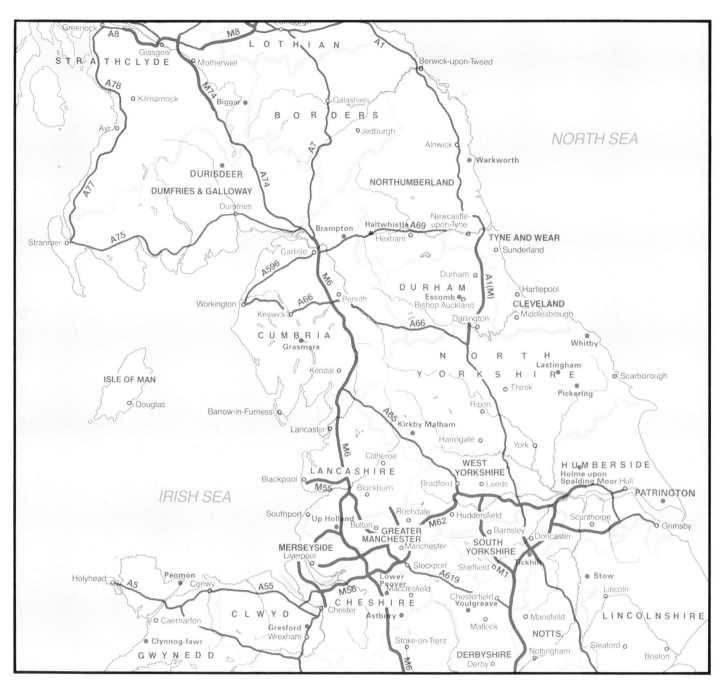

2
Gazetteer

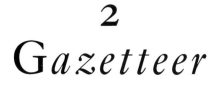

ABBOTTS ANN HAMPSHIRE
ST MARY

Surrounded by magnificent horse-chestnut trees, this church is a gem of mellowed 18th-century brickwork. It has many features typical of the time, seen frequently in London's churches, but less often in the countryside – the stone quoins of the brick walls and the shallow curved top of the windows are typical 'classical' features.

The village was at one time held by Hyde Abbey (hence its name) and in 1716 the church was rebuilt at the expense of one of the Pitt family, forebear of the famous statesman.

It is one of those few churches to remain largely unaltered by the Victorians. The odour of polish from its original woodwork greets you. The squire's pew is a box pew, or rather a set of them, with a small central pew almost imprisoned by the others. Box pews were built not for keeping the fidgets in, but the draughts out – there was no church heating until the 19th century.

There are Victorian additions, in the shape of stained glass in some windows (which is rather out of keeping with the restrained simplicity of the church), and the organ, which is much too large for its position in the chancel. Tracery on the easternmost round windows is also Victorian. But if these features can be ignored, the Georgian atmosphere is undamaged.

This church maintained the medieval tradition of virgins' crowns. A crown, rather like a small candelabrum of hazelwood decorated with paper rosettes, was carried at the

Left The south porch at Ewelme in Oxfordshire

funeral of an unmarried person of good character and then hung high on the side wall of the nave, to decay and fall in time. The oldest here is of 1740 and commemorates one John Morant. Others commemorated are named on the pew kneelers, embroidered in recent years.

About 2 miles (3 km) south-west of
Andover, to the west of the A343 to
Salisbury (map page 57)

ASHTON DEVON
ST JOHN THE BAPTIST

Set on the slopes above the village, this very attractive church was rebuilt during the years 1400 to 1485. It has wagon roofs and other features typical of West Country Perpendicular wool churches.

The south door is scarred by bullet holes made during the Civil War, in 1646. Inside, the full glory of the church is revealed. The arcades are of a white chalk from the cliffs at Beer to the south-east of Exeter, and the walls are plastered. Ancient colour glows from the window glass, some of which has heraldic devices, and from the wall paintings on the north wall of the Lady Chapel, which show Christ and the instruments of his Passion. The 15th-century screen across the chancel entrance, and that which closes off the Lady Chapel, are also beautifully coloured.

Figures painted on the screen panels include saints, and the Virgin and Child. Those of the parclose are particularly interesting. They are larger than those of the rood screen and show Old Testament prophets with inscribed scrolls streaming behind them. They rather resemble woodcuts and may have been taken from a pattern book. This habit of painting the panels of screens is typical of both Devon and East Anglia.

The Jacobean pulpit has a carved tester, or sounding board, above, designed to throw the preacher's voice down to the congregation.

7 miles (11 km) south-west of Exeter,
just off the B3193, 3 miles (5 km) north
of the A38 (map page 56)

◆

ASHWELL HERTFORDSHIRE
St Mary

This 14th-century church has a grand west tower, rising magnificently in four distinct storeys. It is faced in clunch, a hard form of chalk that would have been dug locally. There are various items of interest to be seen before entering: the 15th-century lych gate is one of the few double gates in Britain; the south porch has what were originally priests' rooms above (one has since been demolished), and the original main doors retain their iron strappings and sanctuary ring.

The church is spacious and well lit, with little or no stained glass. There are 15th-century sedilia and a fine carved screen to the Lady Chapel in the south aisle. The style of the pillars shows development from east to west, for – as was customary – the chancel was begun (1340) before the nave (finished in 1380). So this building work spanned the period of the Great Plague, and it is for messages from that stricken time that this church is so famous.

On the north wall of the tower are various graffiti and drawings. One 12 ft (3.5 m) from the floor runs:
Primula pestis in M ter CCC fuit L minus uno
'The first plague was in 1000, 300 and 50 minus 1' – that is, 1349.

Then 3 ft (1 m) below, deeply cut in Old English lettering, the bottom part reads:

The 14th-century church at Ashwell

MCCCL superest plebs pessima testis in fine qe̅ ventus validus hoc anno Maurus in orbe tonat MCCC LXI
This can be translated: '1350 the dregs of the people live to tell the tale and in the end a mighty wind / this year Maurus thunders in the heavens 1361' (St Maurus' Day was 15 January).

Within the tower is a unique drawing of Old St Paul's in London, with the central tower and lofty spire destroyed in the Great Fire of 1666 (see page 34). Architectural features shown date it to the 14th or 15th century – it was perhaps drawn by someone fleeing the plague which preceded the Great Fire.

1 mile (1.5 km) to the north of the A505
between Royston and Baldock
(map page 57)

◆

ASTBURY CHESHIRE
St Mary

This magnificent, battlemented church is largely Perpendicular in style, but as is so often the case, earlier churches had stood here before that great rebuilding. The

Moreton chapel at the east end of the north aisle is the chancel of the Early English church of about 1240.

The 15th-century church was built slightly further to the south, leaving the original Norman tower (now refaced and with a spire added probably in Decorated times) as a separate belfry tower standing almost apart. The tower rising over the grand western porch is a peel tower, with refuge rooms for women and children when Welsh raiders were abroad, or which might also be used by chantry priests. In the porch, the ceremony of exorcism which preceded baptism took place, and among the carvings is a devil raging at the rescue of a soul. There is also a very elaborate south porch, with a priest's room above, which stores such oddments as a fragment of old tiled pavement, a vestment chest and 'frying pan' collecting boxes.

The church is spacious within. There are two major items of interest. The first is the 15th-century rood screen, which rises to a spread of elegant tracery. The second is the beautifully carved and painted group of ceilings to the nave and aisles; that to the south includes 51 horned devils and a fox

The church at Astbury is largely Perpendicular

preaching to geese. This last is a fairly common motif found on bench ends, misericords and such situations. Presumably then as now, the fox is sly, the geese silly – an odd notion for a church, though a standard medieval allegory.

The 15th-century stone lych gate is also of interest.

9 miles (14.5 km) north of Newcastle
under Lyme, on the A34
(map pages 57–8).

BARNACK CAMBRIDGESHIRE
ST JOHN THE BAPTIST

There have been at least four phases of building at Barnack: Saxon, Early English, Decorated and Perpendicular. Saxon work is still seen on the lowest two stages of its tower in the shape of long-and-short work, pilaster strips, windows with triangular heads and some slabs in the tower walls, carved with foliage. It is bulky, and may have acted as the nave of the original 11th-century Saxon church.

The tower's Early English upper storey is dated to around 1200, with contemporary windows, and a short octagonal spire. Much of the nave also dates from 1200, while the chancel is 14th-century, its east window having Decorated tracery. The chapel to the south of the chancel is 15th-century Perpendicular.

There is a small recess in the west wall of the tower, with a triangular head. Some people say it is Saxon, perhaps a seat in which the thegn, or local lord, sat while adjudicating; others maintain that it is medieval and of unknown use.

The church has two treasures. The lesser is the Decorated font, looking like an iced cake on a stand of trefoil arches. The greater is a late Saxon carving of Christ in Majesty. It is a sophisticated masterpiece, reflecting manuscript illuminations of the time, in the pose and in the way the drapery falls.

3 miles (5 km) east of Stamford, on the
B1443 (map page 57)

BISHOPSTONE WILTSHIRE
St John the Baptist

Elegantly set, this cruciform church with a crossing tower has many Decorated features. The transepts and chancel have tall, two-light windows with simple 'flowing' tracery – resembling the centre of a fleur-de-lis. The south window of the south transept has reticulated tracery.

Outside, below this window, there is a unique, two-bay, vaulted 'cloister' with Decorated arches. It contains a tomb chest, ornamented with ballflowers, which may be a monument to the patron who added the transept. It was perhaps built in rivalry to the immense founder's monument which stands in the north transept. Both south and north doorways have Decorated mouldings, although the two-storeyed porch is Perpendicular.

The interior of the east end of the church matches the interest of the exterior, with rib vaulting in the chancel and south transept. There are ornate sedilia and piscinas, and interesting monuments, including one of about 1630 to a divine, and a mid 19th-century Gothic example by Augustus Welby Pugin.

5 miles (8 km) south-west of Salisbury,
2 miles (3 km) off the A354 at Coombe
Bissett (map page 57)

◆

BLANDFORD FORUM DORSET
St Peter and St Paul

The original church was destroyed in 1731, when fire swept through the town centre. It was rebuilt in 1733–9 by a local family of architects as a noble Palladian edifice. It seems somewhat cramped by its surroundings, because it keeps to the site of its predecessor.

Behind the west portal rises a tall, square tower, at the top of which is a cupola set behind balustrades, with an urn at each corner. The pedimented western portico is echoed by others on the north and south sides.

Left *The Palladian church at Blandford Forum*

Inside it is a satisfying example of its time. Giant Ionic columns rise to an ornamental plaster ceiling. It almost entirely escaped the heavy hand of Victorian restoration and keeps its original font, a pulpit in Grinling Gibbons style from a London church, box pews, and a splendid mayoral seat of 1748, set like a throne with an imposing cover.

It was customary at that time to erect a gallery across the west end of the nave for singers, musician and organ. The Victorians moved the organ, originally installed in 1794, down towards the chancel – but it was moved back in 1970. In fact, the only lasting major change made in Victorian times occurred in 1895, when the curved, apsidal sanctuary was moved (on rollers) to the east to allow a chancel to be inserted between it and the nave.

On the A354, 23 miles (37 km) south of
Salisbury (map pages 56–7)

◆

BLISLAND CORNWALL
St Protus and St Hyacinth

Dotted with ancient stones and settlements, the whole of this area reeks of the past. Of Cornwall's 260 wayside crosses, seven are in Blisland. Most of these were erected in the pre-Christian era, but the early missionary Church appropriated them by carving the cross on them. The church at Blisland is dedicated to two brothers who were martyred in Italy and whose relics are preserved there. Why they were adopted here is not known.

The nave is Norman, and one of the fonts, recovered from the churchyard, is also of that time. The church was transformed in the 15th century, when the tower (which is, unusually, sited north of the north transept), porch, aisles and transepts were added. The tower and porch are both made of blocks of local granite.

The church was intelligently restored at the end of the 19th century. The splendid wagon roofs with their carved bosses were retained. A medieval-style rood screen was designed, and a Renaissance-style high altar and other features – all exuberantly coloured – were added. The screen

carries a rood, a crucifix with Christ suffering, with attendant figures of Mary and St John the Baptist. Other items of furniture range from a 1662 communion table below the screen, to the 20th-century reredos in the Lady Chapel. Although a jumble of dates and styles, Blisland does echo the visual vitality of a medieval church before it was laid to waste during Reformation and Puritan times. The fine Jacobean pulpit, carved in the manner of Grinling Gibbons with flowered, hanging swags, is worth a journey in itself.

4 miles (6.5 km) north-east of Bodmin,
1 mile (1.5 km) north of the A30
(map page 56)

BOTTESFORD LEICESTERSHIRE
ST MARY

This is one of the largest village churches in England. The 210 ft (64 m) high spire, decorated with crockets, and the imposing nave are 15th-century, but parts of the chancel date from the late 12th and 13th centuries. Above the Victorian royal coat of arms on the chancel arch are the remnants of a medieval Doom painting. The 'wine glass' pulpit (on a thin stem) of 1631 is interesting, but the church is noted principally for the burial monuments of families who occupied Belvoir Castle. Almost filling the chancel, they show how armour, clothing and memorials changed through five centuries.

The oldest effigy is in Purbeck 'marble' (a dark limestone) and dates from 1285. It was brought here from a nearby abbey during the Dissolution of the Monasteries. By the vestry door is an inscribed heart-stone from the same abbey – the heart was often brought home to be buried, if the person died far away. By the time of the tomb of 1414, alabaster, which is easy to carve and colour when fresh but hardens with time, had become popular: Sir William de Roos is dressed in a mixture of chain and plate armour. On the tomb

The church at Blisland, alongside the village green

67

of his son John, Lord Roos, who died in 1421, the plate armour is more complete.

By the 16th century, the individuals commemorated were more accurately depicted, a reflection of the increased importance of 'likeness' in portraits. This is shown by the tomb of the first Earl of Rutland, who died in 1543 and was the first to be buried actually within this church rather than moved here.

The 1563 monument to the second Earl is unusual in that he and the Countess lie underneath a table with carved legs, which may symbolize a communion table of Elizabethan, Reformation times. In the monument of 1588, the fourth Earl wears less armour and by that of 1632, the sixth Earl is depicted in court dress. This massive memorial, with 'classical' touches in such things as the pillars, shows his two wives and children. According to an inscription, the two sons both 'died in their infancy by wicked practice and sorcerye'.

The seventh Earl died in 1641, but his tomb was not built until 1684, at the same time as the eighth Earl's (who died in 1676), and is thought to be by Grinling Gibbons. The marble statue of the seventh Earl shows him standing in Roman dress, a fashion in funeral monuments which started in about 1660, and lasted for around a century.

7 miles (11 km) west of Grantham on
the A52 (map page 57)

———————◆———————

BRADFIELD BERKSHIRE
St Andrew

Sir Gilbert Scott, a well-known Victorian church architect and restorer, helped the rector and the lord of the manor to rebuild this church in the 1840s. He included echoes of Transitional and Gothic styles with ideas taken from churches in neighbouring villages. The chancel alone would mark it as an ambitious work. Longer than the nave, it is impressive both in scale and detail – in such things as the ironwork screens and the candelabra by the altar.

Some of the original church was kept, notably the north arcade with its 14th-century pillars and arches (the larger arch at the end of the north aisle, above the organ, is the original chancel arch). It is interesting to compare this north arcade with the 19th-century imitation to the south. The chevron-decorated arch between the choir and the south transept is inspired by a 12th-century arch in Aldermaston (Berkshire). The sanctuary arch, with one order of deep-cut lozenge design and another of a choir of angels, is unique – although vaguely reminiscent of one at Sonning (Oxfordshire).

An example of the Victorian adaptation of the Gothic style is seen in the group of four lancet windows in the south aisle. The wall is massively thick and the short windows are deeply splayed (the walls cut away) and decorated on the inside. Massive walls with splayed windows are a Saxon feature, but lancets are Early English. Windows would neither have been grouped nor decorated in this way in a medieval church – yet the assemblage looks 'Gothic'.

The timbering of the nave roof links with that of this south aisle in an unusual way, giving a view of the aisle from the nave – another imaginative touch.

There is a poignant bronze plaque on the south wall of the south transept, a memorial to the wife of Reverend Thomas Stevens, who had this church rebuilt, after she had died young in 1840.

3 miles (5 km) west of the edge of
Reading, north of the A4 (map page 57)

———————◆———————

BRADFORD ON AVON WILTSHIRE
St Lawrence

St Aldhelm is thought to have erected a church here in around AD 700, but the present structure was built in the 10th century, after Viking raids. The little church was rediscovered in 1871, having served as a barn. Its features had been hidden by later walling, which has since been removed. It is of simple two-cell plan, with a nave and a square-ended chancel or sanctuary (see illustration on page 11). There was a porticus to the north and another to the

The square-ended Saxon church at Bradford on Avon

south, but only the former remains.

Except for some blind arcading and pilaster strips the outside is plain. Inside it is tall and lean, lit dimly by round-headed windows and the light coming in through the doorway. The openings between the nave and chancel and porticus are narrow, less than 3 ft (1 m) wide, with crude 'capitals' from which the arches spring.

The church has an atmospheric interior, its stonework primitive although finely cut and jointed. It lacks decoration, except for some rolls alongside the porticus entrance and two carved angels high above the chancel arch. They are Byzantine in style, carrying drapes over their arms to catch the blood of Christ. They presumably remain from a rood assembly. Relics of a Saxon cross and altar frontal have been placed in the chancel.

**Bradford on Avon is about 5 miles
(8 km) south-east of Bath, on the A363
(map pages 56–7)**

BRAMPTON CUMBRIA
St Martin

This 'jittery and jumpy masterpiece' of a church was finished in 1878. One of those patrons who had pledged his cash wished 'it had been for a better cause than that precious warehouse of a place'. The architect, Philip Webb, said later that he had designed his church 'for somewhat unliftable citizens of a really mean north country town. . . .'

It was not, of course, Brampton's first church – a predecessor stands on the site of a Roman fort $1\frac{1}{2}$ miles (2.5 km) to the west; recently restored, with echoes of Celtic Christianity, it is worth a diversion. By the 18th century, the almshouse chapel was serving as parish church, but in the 1870s a dynamic vicar led a campaign for a new church rather than the proposed new-fangled tramway.

The church shows scant regard for what was thought to be the 'correct style' promoted by the ecclesiologists. Its two aisles are quite different from each other. And their roofs are unusual: the north aisle has a wooden tunnel vault; the south, a lean-to. The nave ceiling is flat, but with a fake springing above each pillar. Its layout incorporated the Low or Broad Church views of the vicar, with an open interior, having no real separate chancel and no pulpit (one of the clergy stalls almost in the centre of the church performed this function).

The stained glass is of international importance. It was designed by William Morris and Sir Edward Burne-Jones, two of the group of Pre-Raphaelites who brought creative art to interior decoration. Drawn cartoons might be used in many different churches with different colours, but the windows here are all from original designs, the themes being worship, heroes of the Bible, virtues and innocent childhood. Burne-Jones joked about the east window in his account book: 'a masterpiece of style, a *chef d'oeuvre* of invention, a *capo d'opera* of conception . . . hastily estimated in a moment of generous friendship for £200. . . .'

**7 miles (11 km) north-east of Carlisle,
on the A69 (map page 58)**

Guided Tour

BREAMORE HAMPSHIRE
ST MARY

This large, practically complete 10th-century Saxon church stands at the edge of Breamore Park, ten minutes' walk down a narrow lane from today's village. The path from the south gate of the churchyard passes an ancient yew tree. Nearby are stone coffins, brought from a nearby priory suppressed during the Dissolution of the Monasteries, in 1536. The rough walls of the church contain unbroken flint nodules, perhaps raided from a nearby Roman villa – for among them are fragments of red Roman tiles. These walls were probably originally

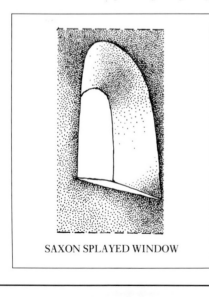

SAXON SPLAYED WINDOW

plastered smooth, and perhaps whitewashed. A squat tower is stationed between nave and chancel.

Before entering the church, make a detour eastwards to the south 'transept'. Its corners are strengthened by massive, typically Saxon long-and-short work. At waist-height on the south-east corner is a primitive sundial: two scratched lines monitored the shadow cast by a stick rammed in the hole above. Also typically Saxon is the double splayed east window of this 'transept', with the opening set half-way into the thick wall which is cut back both inside and outside.

This is not a true transept, as would have been built in Norman and later times to integrate with the height of nave and chancel. It is merely a side chapel built on to the central tower; its matching companion on the north side of the tower no longer exists.

The porch was built in two stages. Its lower part is 12th-century, as are the doorway and the round carved medallion of the Lamb of God above it. The upper part (which was once floored) is 15th-century, and was presumably added to protect the carved Saxon rood set into the wall over the doorway. This was moved here from its original position over the arch in the east end of the nave when that (and the chancel arch) were enlarged in

the 15th century. Although defaced during the Reformation, the outline of Christ is still visible.

We enter the church on to a stone-flagged floor, below a western gallery which was added after the storms of the Reformation had abated. It was for the choir and musicians who had earlier used the rood loft. An organ of a later date is here – a typical addition. The arch at the east end of the nave (the west wall of the tower) and the chancel arch are both 15th-century, and very handsome, with beautifully carved foliage touches – showing thistles, acorns and oak leaves, and grapes and vine leaves. The wood-framed upper doorway to the missing rood loft can be seen to the north side of the nave arch. This arch leads to the tower, where bell ropes hang down. The bells were originally rung from a floor 15 ft (4.5 m) above.

The doorway leading to the south 'transept' or chapel that we have already inspected outside is of great interest. Note that it is merely a doorway, and not a true archway as would have been built later. The Anglo-Saxon inscription cut into the arch, HER SWUTELATH SEO GECWYDRAEDNES THE, can be translated 'Here is made plain the word to thee'. The unusual 'cable' carving on the two blocks of stone supporting the arch at each side may have come from the nearby Roman villa. Inside this side chapel (now the vestry) we see the interior splay of the Saxon window noted earlier. There are six similar windows in this church.

The chancel was rebuilt in the 14th century on the Saxon foundations. Its east window – notably the only pointed

(Gothic) window here – has Decorated tracery. The old chest in the chancel has three locks – three separate keys were needed to open it, held by three different

St Mary's at Breamore shows clearly its Saxon heritage ; the south porticus with its Saxon windows is a prominent feature

persons. This was the usual practice – scarcely a sign of trust!

On the north chancel wall towards its west end are traces of a low window. Many churches have one here, or signs of one, and various explanations are popular. They are sometimes (mistakenly) referred to as 'lepers' windows', but it was common in medieval times for an anchorite's (hermit's) cell – perhaps a simple wattled

hut – to be built against the outside wall of the chancel, and this window could give the devotee sight of the altar. At COMPTON (Surrey) skeletons were found on the site of such a hut, underlining the fact that hermits took their vows until death.

To the west of the A338, half-way between Salisbury and Ringwood (map page 57)

BRENT KNOLL SOMERSET
ST MICHAEL

Churches dedicated to the Archangel Michael are often found on a knoll, like this one, or other high point; some suspect that with the arrival of Christianity, St Michael replaced a pagan god who was often associated with hilltops (see also BRENTOR, Devon).

The building is largely 15th-century Perpendicular. The tower is a fine example of that time, with three belfry windows abreast, although only the central one is pierced, those to either side being 'blind'.

The interior of the roof is a striking example of camber-beam construction, divided underneath into square panels ornamented with carved tracery. But it is the bench ends for which this church is rightly known. A famous trio ridicules the church authorities. The first shows a fox disguised as an abbot, preaching to pigs in cowls (presumably monks) and birds (the ordinary parishioners); below his feet demons, looking rather like monkeys, roast a pig on a spit. In the next, the fox's secret is discovered and he is stripped of his mitre and placed in the stocks. In the third, he is hanged by the birds.

A brightly coloured memorial of 1663 to John Somerset and two wives is also of interest. The wives sport very different head-dresses; tombs like this illustrate fashions, which could change as quickly then as they do today.

About 6 miles (9.5 km) south of Weston
super Mare, off the B3140 to the west of
the A38 (map page 56)

◆

BRENTOR DEVON
ST MICHAEL

Perched on the plug of an extinct volcano, and with views to Dartmoor, Plymouth Sound, Bodmin Moor and Exmoor, this church attracts many visitors.

There are more than 800 churches dedicated to St

Left *The spectacular hilltop location of Brentor*

Michael in Britain, and many are located on high ground, sometimes on a pinnacle such as this – the ruined chapel at Roche in Cornwall is another example. Churches were sometimes built on pagan sites, which (to save argument and smooth the path to conversion) the Christian Church adopted and renamed. The hill here is enclosed by the banks of an Iron Age hillfort, but this was more of a stronghold than a religious site.

Some think that such high-standing churches were 'beacon' churches, the warning brazier standing on top of the tower. Folk traditions grew (or were invented by Victorian antiquarians), and one has it that Brentor church was first built at the bottom of the hill, but was moved to the top by the devil to deter worshippers.

A land charter shows that the first church here was erected in about 1130, but rebuilt early in the 13th century with the tower added or remodelled in the 15th. It is a small church (the fourth smallest in England), and is now only used during the summer months. Its low, thick walls are pierced with what seem to be simple and early windows, and has a very plain interior. It was restored from a very dilapidated state at the end of the 19th century. The undecorated octagonal font, although of uncertain age, is perhaps the oldest relic, while the stone sundial on the south side of the tower (with its quaint half-imp-half-angel figure) is dated to 1694.

5 miles (8 km) north of Tavistock, west
of the A386 and south of North Brentor
village (map page 56)

◆

BRIXWORTH NORTHAMPTONSHIRE
ALL SAINTS

Many people count this as Britain's finest Anglo-Saxon church. It was originally part of a 7th-century monastic complex, but this was plundered by Vikings (fire-reddened stone can be seen high up on the west end of the north wall) and it eventually came to serve a small village, which helped to keep it from being vandalized.

73

The fine Saxon church of Brixworth

It was originally of basilican plan, with a nave and chancel, which had at its end a polygonal apse. Along each side of the nave was a row of porticus, side chapels reached through arched doorways. With the porticus gone, the arches can now be seen on the outside walls, blocked in but pierced by smaller windows, and the first on the south wall contains a plain Norman doorway. The reused Roman tiles which head the Saxon arches catch the eye; there is little of Roman order in the way they are set!

The top of the western tower and its spire were raised on the Saxon tower-porch which also had side porticus; the round stair turret is also Saxon, but from the 10th century.

Within the church, the great arch at the end of the nave dates from about 1400. It replaced a triple arch which was probably a larger version of that high on the west wall of the nave. This gives a view into the nave from an upper chamber in the tower, which was normally used by Saxons of rank as a private chapel.

By the pulpit, in an iron cage, is a reliquary which was discovered in a wall of the Lady Chapel in 1820, containing a small piece of bone. This may be the relic of St Boniface (who died in AD 757) which was traditionally associated with the church. The church had another peculiar feature, namely a sunken ring crypt which circled a crypt chapel beneath the apse. This would have housed the relic, the ring crypt allowing pilgrims to view it during their devotions.

7 miles (11 km) north of Northampton,
on the A508 (map page 57)

BURFORD OXFORDSHIRE
St John the Baptist

This cruciform church developed from a Norman one, of which such parts as the central tower and the doorway with beakheads and chevron moulding remain. The somewhat haphazard growth has resulted in a cluster of oddly angled aisles and chapels. There is much 15th-century work, for this parish was in one of the prime wool areas. The porch, the chapels alongside the chancel, and the top of the tower date from that time.

As the bare stone testifies, the inside has been scraped clean of plaster and heavily restored in Victorian times – and proudly, as the inscriptions testify. However, its 'skinning alive' led William Morris, the Victorian poet, artist and craftsman, to start an 'antiscrape' movement which became the Society for the Protection of Ancient Buildings, Britain's first amenity society.

There are interesting memorials: formal ones such as the Tanfield tomb in the north aisle (there is a skeleton beneath the couple's bed) and the brasses of merchant folk; and informal, such as the scratching 'ANTHONY SEDLEY 1649 PRISNER' on the lead font lining – written by a young mutineer who was held here by Cromwell. Bells, cast in

1635, are displayed in the north transept.

In the churchyard are fine examples of local box 'bale tombs', representing bales of wool. Some with a skull symbolize a shroud – at that time it was compulsory to be buried in a woollen shroud to help the wool trade.

18 miles (29 km) west of Oxford, on the
A40 (map page 57)

CAREW CHERITON DYFED
(DEDICATION UNKNOWN)

A diversion to Carew is worthwhile for a number of reasons. The church itself is largely 13th- to 15th-century, and has several fine features, such as the tower with its corner steeple, and the chancel floor tiles dated 1500, which are decorated with heraldic ravens. There are also some interesting memorials, including one of the 14th century, depicting a small girl whose hands enfold a heart.

There is also a chapel in the churchyard. This was in fact an *ossuary* or charnel house, in which the bones of the dead were stored. In areas where the bedrock lay not far from the surface, it was often necessary to clear the graveyard from time to time for new burials, the older bones being stored in the charnel house. Only the skull and two long bones were kept, as the minimum necessary to ensure resurrection. The 'skull and crossbones' are sometimes seen carved on a tombstone. The Carew Cheriton charnel house is contemporary with the church, but was used as a school in the 16th and 17th centuries.

Most visitors will also go to see Carew Castle a mile away. Near its entrance stands a tall, 14 ft (4 m) high Celtic cross decorated with plaits and knotwork. It carries the inscription 'MARGITEUT REX ETG. FILI' – Mareddud son of King Edwin. He was killed in 1035.

4 miles (6.5 km) east of Pembroke, at the
junction of the A477 and A4075 (map page 56)

The Norman doorway at Burford

CLAYPOLE LINCOLNSHIRE
ST PETER

The beautiful proportions of this church belie the fact that it was built not at one time, but over 200 years and in a number of phases.

The earliest parts of this building are from the 13th-century church, which replaced an earlier (probably wooden) Saxon one. The lower stages of the tower are Early English, and date from about 1225. In the south transept, parts of a separate Lady Chapel appear to have been incorporated, since the sedilia, west window, double piscina and south doorway date from about 1275, while the rest are from about 1325.

At this time, the old nave was demolished and replaced

by one with aisles and a tall clerestory; a third stage was added to the tower, and a slightly smaller north transept and a chancel were built. This is all beautiful Decorated work, especially the naturalistic carving of the capitals in the nave arcades, which is among the best of this period to be seen in Britain. Oak, bryony, hawthorn and grapevine can be recognized. On some of the capitals is the face of a 'green man', peeping through the foliage. He was a survival from pre-Christian mythology, linked with May Day celebrations and with hawthorn (which flowers in May).

In about 1375, the chancel was enlarged and the sacristy added on its north side. This part of the building marks the transition between Decorated and Perpendicular architecture, and the three-seated sedilia in the south wall of the chancel is exquisite.

In the early 15th century the fourth stage and parapet spire were added to the western tower; the 'battlements' and the south porch to the nave were added at this time, too. The door has carved panelling and tracery, handmade nails and an unusual, small wicket door. Many of the corbels supporting the nave battlements are of heads and figures; some are beautiful and some quite grotesque.

The evolving architectural styles of the building are echoed in the furniture, notably in the 14th-century Decorated tracery of the font and the 15th-century Perpendicular ornament of the pulpit.

5 miles (8 km) south-east of Newark,
east of the A1 (map page 57)

CLYNNOG-FAWR GWYNEDD
St Beuno

This is a mainly late 15th-century building, a sturdy but beautiful example of 'rustic' Perpendicular; even the acerbic Samuel Johnson had a good word for it. 'It is very spacious and magnificent for this country', he wrote in 1774. However, such things as the arched tracery heads to the windows make it English in style — Welsh masons would have carved rectangular tracery heads. It has been cleared

The 'rustic' Perpendicular church at Clynnog-fawr

of its Victorian pews, and looks the better for this. There is fine woodwork in the nave roof, a restored screen and other features.

It was a magnet for pilgrims – those en route for the Celtic holy place of Bardsey Island assembled here, and it also held a shrine to St Beuno. Nothing of this remains, but one tradition has it that he is buried below the chapel, which lies to the south-west, and which possibly marks the site of his own oratory. Tradition also links his name with the chest hollowed out of one piece of timber, preserved in the glass case behind the main door. Until the 19th century, calves or lambs born with the mark of St Beuno – slit or notched ears – were offered to the churchwardens to sell, the proceeds being stored in this chest along with the offerings of pilgrims and donations made by confessed sinners.

There is an odd item of interest – namely the pair of dog tongs in the south transept, made of iron with short spikes for securing a quarrelsome animal. Well into the 19th century, people took their dogs to church with them, perhaps as foot warmers.

On the A499, about 10 miles (16 km)
south-west of Caernarfon
(map page 58)

COMPTON SURREY
St Nicholas

This is a typical example of a Saxon church extended and largely rebuilt by the Normans. Saxon work remains in the west tower, with its sturdy cornering, although the shingled broach spire which caps it is 14th-century.

Both doorways are Norman: the north door appears to have sunk – the ground level in the churchyard has risen as a result of innumerable burials over the course of the centuries. The south doorway is now protected by a modern porch.

There are Transitional features inside, including the arcades which follow the line of the original Saxon walls. Their simple arches are not quite round but as yet barely pointed.

On the chancel arch is what looks like a mason's mark of five rings, and the scratched figure of a knight, who can be dated to the 12th century by his helmet. Above this arch is an intriguing Norman painted mural – a witty optical illusion. It is a pattern of steps which seem to change direction at the blink of an eye, and may signify the perilous climb to heaven.

The upper chapel above the sanctuary is unique. It still has its original Norman wooden screen. It was perhaps used by pilgrims on the Pilgrims' Way to Canterbury which runs not far away. (In the splay of the Norman window in the Lady Chapel are cut some typical pilgrims' crosses.)

Below the upper chapel, in the east window of the sanctuary, is a deliciously coloured stained-glass image of the Virgin and Child, which may be the oldest in Britain. It is of unknown origin. The small window in the north chancel wall was probably designed to allow an anchorite or anchoress, immured in a cell outside, a view of the altar. Six skeletons were found on the site in 1906.

About 3 miles (5 km) south-west of
Guildford, just off the A3
(map page 57)

COPFORD GREEN ESSEX
St Michael and All Angels

The church's appearance is charming, with its short wooden bell turret and short spire perched atop a deep roof. It is basically Norman, built in around 1130 to a very simple plan of aisleless nave and apsidal sanctuary. The courses of different coloured stone in the north wall, which is original, are said to resemble those in the walls of Constantinople.

A chapel was added at the eastern end of the south wall in about 1190, and this was extended westward to make an aisle, with the original wall pierced through, about a century later. The south aisle wall contains some early medieval bricks, which are perhaps the first to be made locally since Roman times. The three windows in the apse are from the original building, the others restored or added later. The roof of the nave once had a loft lit by the top windows in the west front. The timber roof dates from about 1400.

The fame of the church lies in the 12th-century wall paintings covering the original walls. The paintings transform the church. True, some have been rather obviously 'restored' – compare the Christ in Majesty in the apse with the untouched picture of the Raising of Jairus' Daughter above the window which lights the pulpit. This warmly, but

The church at Copford Green is largely Norman

dramatically, shows the dying girl, weeping mother, anxious father and loving Christ.

The paintings probably date from around 1150, with dress and armour showing details of that time. They were obliterated with whitewash during the Reformation, uncovered during repairs in 1690, but whited over again, and remained hidden until 1871. A programme of repair and conservation work to protect the building and paintings is in hand.

In the 12th century and later medieval days, flaying – alive or after hanging – seems to have been a penalty for sacrilege. The skin was then apparently nailed to the church door as a warning to others. The old south door (now in the north entrance) had some leathery pieces of hide – apparently human – between the wood and iron, which are now kept locked away.

About 4 miles (6.5 km) south-west of
Colchester, just south of the A12
(map page 57)

CROSCOMBE SOMERSET
St Mary

Pinnacles, parapets, windows and a wagon roof are among the clues that this church was rebuilt in the 15th century. It is largely Perpendicular in style, although the graceful Early English doorway of the south porch, for example, remains from the earlier church. It has a fine spire. There is one unusual feature – the two-storey treasury with iron-grilled windows added to the south-west corner in around 1500. The Guilds of Croscombe – *the Young Men, the Maidens, the Weavers, the Fullers, the Hogglers* (labourers), *the Archers* and *the Wives* – met here; it was later used as the parish armoury and at one time as the parish lockup!

Some of these guilds were like 'friendly' societies. They may have set up chantries, private enclosures, within the church, where masses were said to release guildmembers' souls from purgatory. The Reformation stamped on what was seen as 'superstitious nonsense', and took down the old

rood and often its screen. This church, however, was refurnished in the early 17th century, and is famous for its complete set of Jacobean furnishings.

The rood screen was allowed again in 1561, under Elizabeth I, to solve the problem of using a medieval church for prayer book worship. Before the Reformation, the villagers were restricted to the nave; the Reformed Church used the screen to separate different areas for different parts of the services. Here an ornate screen of 1620 replaces the medieval version which had been destroyed. It carries the Royal Arms of James I instead of the rood.

The pulpit, also a fine piece of carving, has a carved tester above to reflect the sermon down to the congregation on the benches and in the box pews (also known as dozing pens) below. Some of the 15th-century pews have survived, with typical 'poppyheads' rising at the ends.

3 miles (4.5 km) east of Wells, on the
A371 (map pages 56–7)

CULBONE SOMERSET
St Beuno

It is a short but worthwhile pilgrimage to this tiny church set in woodland by a rocky stream, in an Exmoor combe 400 ft (122 m) above the Bristol Channel nearby. It is best reached on foot, a walk of a mile or so.

The Guinness Book of Records claims it as the smallest church in England – an average congregation of a dozen plus organist (lit by candles, as there is no electricity) seems just right. Nave and chancel together are no more than 35 ft (10.5 m) long and 12 to 13 ft (less than 4 m) wide. The thick rubble walls may be 12th-century or earlier (the lofty nave does suggest a Saxon origin) and the window in the north wall of the chancel – two lights cut from a single slab of stone with (outside) a little, shallow-cut face – may well be Saxon. The pointed chancel arch, however, is Gothic, probably a 13th-century replacement of the Norman original. The porch dates from the same period. Other windows were inserted in later years, and the slate-covered spire was erected in 1810. The churchyard cross was added to an old base (possibly from the 15th century) in 1966.

The plain white interior with its rood screen, dated 1400, and simple 12th-century font is a delight. The seating does not detract from the simplicity; some seats date from the 15th century.

St Beuno was one of a band of Celtic missionaries who crossed from Wales and Ireland in the late 6th century; he died in AD 623, and traditionally has strong links with the Celtic stronghold of Bardsey Island. Near Culbone stables is a Bronze Age standing stone with a wheel cross cut on it, one radius extending to point down towards the church. This stone is one of several waymarking an ancient track, and suggests that St Beuno's was a place of pilgrimage, but what relic it held is not known. (See also CLYNNOG-FAWR, Gwynedd.) Many country churches were in fact well-visited places of pilgrimage in medieval times, with shrines containing relics of the saint. Few such shrines survived the Reformation, however.

**10 miles (16 km) west of Minehead,
north of the A39 (map page 56)**

The tiny church of St Beuno at Culbone

CULLOMPTON DEVON
ST ANDREW

The church was built in 1430, with a continuous nave and chancel (there is no chancel arch between them), flanked with aisles. The tower and Lane's Aisle were added early in the 16th century. Lane's Aisle is a chantry chapel to a local clothier, John Lane, which runs alongside the south aisle; the original south wall was removed and replaced by piers and buttresses. There are a few later additions, such as the long Jacobean gallery at the west end of the nave. Although the east end was changed in the 19th century, the building is one of the best 'whole church' examples of Perpendicular style.

There is a magnificent boarded wagon roof which covers both nave and chancel; its arches, ribs and bosses are elaborately carved. It was once ablaze with blue and red, of which only touches remain. A fitting match for this is the rood screen, which reaches across the aisles and nave, coloured in red, blue, green and gold. Its tracery echoes that of the windows and its fan tracery above supports a cornice decorated with vine leaves. Above this is the oak rood beam, which is also elaborately carved.

The Royal Arms now take the place of the rood, but the church's original Golgotha (the base of the rood) now rests in Lane's Aisle: two baulks of timber carved with rocks and skulls, with sockets for the Cross and platforms for the figures of Mary and St John the Baptist.

Lane's Aisle boasts magnificent fan vaulting; the springers are carved with angels holding emblems such as a crown of thorns, spear and wool-related items including sheep shears. The tomb of John Lane and his wife has survived less well; their tomb slab stripped of its brasses lies partly hidden by seating in his fine aisle. Also of great interest are the 32 figures in Tudor dress which decorate the piers along the line of the south aisle wall.

**12 miles (19 km) north-east of Exeter
on the B3181, by junction 28 of the M5
(map page 56)**

The church of St Cuthbert at Dalmeny

DALMENY LOTHIAN
ST CUTHBERT

This church is one of the finest examples of Norman Romanesque in Scotland, or indeed in Britain. Yet all is not quite what it seems. It is thought that it was built in the mid 12th century to a simple plan of western tower, aisleless nave and a square chancel with an apsidal sanctuary at its eastern end. As was often the case, that Norman tower collapsed (probably in the 15th century) and was rebuilt only in the 19th century, while the Rosebery Aisle (really a chapel) was added to the north of the nave in the 17th century, to provide a family 'loft' or pew and burial vault.

From this time pews filled the floor space, and the whole building was reseated in 1816, even the curved apse. The lower parts of chancel and apse arches were cut away to fit the seats. The south wall of the chancel was also pierced by a door and some of the windows were enlarged. This was all made good earlier this century, when the windows were restored to their original size and Norman style, with chevron moulding, and the tower rebuilt. What we see today is a superb restoration.

Of the original Norman features, the south doorway has most impact, with its elaborately carved animals, figures and grotesque heads. Above it is a fine intersecting arcade. But the chevron decoration of the chancel arch is also striking.

Left The fine Perpendicular church at Cullompton

The old stonework also carries a series of mason's marks.

Dalmeny parish provides an example of abuse by Church authorities. The parishioners were serviced by a rector who, although appointed by the landowner, was supported by the parish tithes or 'teinds'. These also paid for the church services and supported the poor. But Jedburgh Abbey was granted the church, and so took the teinds, appointing a vicar to whom they paid only a pittance, leaving the poor to rely on charity. This iniquitous form of taxation on the villagers continued even after the Reformation, as those granted the abbey lands kept the right to the teinds. It was abuses of this kind, however, that were among the root causes of the upheaval of the Reformation.

About 1½ miles (2.5 km) east of the
south end of the Forth Road Bridge,
north of the A90 (map page 59)

◆

DEERHURST GLOUCESTERSHIRE
ST MARY

The first stone church on the site was in place in the 8th century, a simple, tall-walled rectangle, the core of what remains today. This was later given an apse at the east end and three two-storeyed porticus, or small chapels, one at the west end and one either side of the nave near the east end. These porticus remain, although without their upper floors (the best preserved is the south one which extends from today's south aisle). The western one forms the bottom two stages of the tower. The apse was later rebuilt, probably early in the 9th century (part of it remains outside); the blocked-up Saxon sanctuary arch is unusually large for Saxon work. Additional porticus were added running alongside the nave to give separate chapels for saints. Another storey, in fact a separate and important chapel, was eventually added to the tower. Its double window, the most elaborate in any Saxon church, can be seen high in the west wall of the nave. The blank square stone above probably carried a Saxon rood. The tower doorways are of this time.

All of this predates the Norman Conquest. Later, aisles

were added in place of the rows of porticus, the Saxon nave wall was pierced with Early English arches, and a series of clerestory windows was put in.

The fame of the church lies in its Saxon carvings, including the plaque of the Virgin and Child in the tower and the animal heads on the label stops (the ends of the mouldings) over the sanctuary arch and some of the doorways. Deerhurst has one of the finest Saxon fonts in existence, carved with Celtic spirals between borders of vine scroll, a Northumbrian motif. Outside, contained in the surviving arch of the apse is the famous Deerhurst angel – which resembles figures in manuscript illustrations of the time.

The Jacobean pews in the chancel are arranged in the mid 17th-century Puritan fashion around the table, the only example of this system to survive in Britain.

Some 200 yards (180 m) to the south-west is another Saxon building, Odda's Chapel, which is now part of a timber-framed house.

About 8 miles (13 km) north of
Gloucester, to the west of the A38
(map pages 56–7)

◆

DORCHESTER OXFORDSHIRE
St Peter and St Paul

This splendid abbey church was founded on the spot where King Cynegils of Wessex was baptized in AD 634 – a key step in the spread of Christianity. The original Saxon building was replaced by a larger Norman one, and this was largely rebuilt in the 14th century in Decorated style. The western tower was rebuilt in around 1605.

With the Dissolution of the Monasteries, the church was given over to parish use. Until then the parishioners had been restricted to the part of the south aisle which still contains a rood – a wall painting of the crucifixion. In this aisle is a very rare Norman lead font, and also a corbel with a quaint carving of sleeping monks.

The east window is a major feature of the church. Its ornate stone tracery extends down through the whole window (normally it is restricted to the top) and is embellished with carved crockets. The window is, unusually, divided by a vertical buttress from the top of which tracery forms itself into a flower within a circle.

Set into the north wall of the sanctuary is a Jesse window showing the family tree of Christ. In addition to the figures depicted in the glass, the stone tracery has carvings of Old Testament figures. Although Jesus at the top and the Virgin at the bottom were destroyed during the Reformation, most remain. Some of the glass is from the 14th century. Even older, exquisitely coloured 12th-century glass depicting scenes from the life of St Birinus can be seen in the small round windows behind the sedilia in the south wall. This glass is presumably from the previous, Norman east window. Age seems to lend to the colours of such early glass a particular intensity, and they can glow brilliantly. COMPTON (Surrey) contains a similar example.

The 13th-century effigy of a knight in chain mail in the chapel to the south is also unique; he is not resigned in sleep, but vigorously drawing his sword. Outside, there is a preaching cross in the churchyard near the south porch. Nearby is the guest house, the only part of the monastery not destroyed in the Reformation.

About 6 miles (9.5 km) south-east of
the outskirts of Oxford, to the west of
the A423 (map page 57)

◆

EAST HARLING NORFOLK
St Peter and St Paul

'What a riot of wonder!', exclaimed Sir John Betjeman when he visited this church. It is magnificent. There is some 14th-century character, but the main impression is of later Perpendicular style, with large windows, a high clerestory, tall, slender pillars and a fine hammer-beam roof to the nave. This is unusually steeply pitched; some think that this is to echo the angle of fingers touched in prayer. The fine south porch, and the upper tower and its small spire are of this later date.

Continued on page 86

The beautiful Jesse window at Dorchester, showing the family tree of Christ

Guided Tour

DURISDEER DUMFRIES AND GALLOWAY

Durisdeer village nestles snugly in an open bowl of fine hills (the name means 'entrance to the forest'), and trees embrace the ends of the kirkyard. This kirk is a major monument of Scottish Baroque style, and originally had two distinctive leaded ogee'd 'onion'-shaped roofs and a spire above its existing tower.

At the gate to the kirkyard, it is worth pausing to understand the plan. The left (west) wing below the tower looks rather like a house, with its rows of sash windows. Indeed, this part originally held a retiring suite for the laird, and was later used as a school. Now it houses the Sunday School and other church meetings. The main body of the kirk, being T-shaped, is a fine example of post-Reformation Scottish tradition. The stem of the 'T' formed by the south aisle (or wing) points towards the kirkyard gate. This simple plan is obscured, because this south aisle is paired by the Queensberry Aisle on the north side, making a cross.

A sundial to the left of the window above the south door carries the date 1699. Inside the church is light, for the glass is clear and the walls are plain. Yellow pine box pews occupy much of the floor space. They are of mid 19th-century date, with well-made, solid doors. Down the centre of each box runs a narrow 'table'. Elsewhere, open-ended pews are ranked and on many a sloping book board is seen.

There is no altar here; the focus of the church is the pulpit. To its left is attached an 18th-century wrought-iron stand which once held an hour-glass to time the minister's sermon. More recent ironwork also embellishes the church. In front of the pulpit is a table lectern, with three seats behind. In this Presbyterian kirk, no prayer book is used, although the Authorized Version of the Bible is read by the minister.

It is worth climbing to the three lofts (galleries) to see how all the seating has an uninterrupted view of the pulpit. The loft above the south entrance is known as the Duke's Loft; here the members of the Buccleuch family of nearby Drumlanrig Castle sit.

Access to the Queensberry Aisle is through a separate entrance on the kirk's north side. It was part of the original older building, and the new T-shaped kirk was built up against it. The square aisle contains the kirk's most famous Baroque monument – an exuberantly carved tomb in black and white marble of the second Duke of Queensberry and his Duchess. In front of it, poised over the trap door to the family vault, is an elaborate canopy or *baldacchino*, with barley-sugar-twist columns ornamented by trails of foliage.

The kirkyard contains some less grandiose, but perhaps more moving

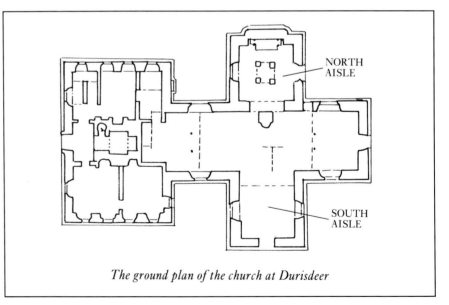

The ground plan of the church at Durisdeer

monuments. Many old gravestones have been built into the east wall of the kirkyard; some carry the rose of Mary, Queen of Scots. And against the south wall of the western wing is set a martyr's

Durisdeer is an example of post-Reformation Scottish tradition

grave. A Covenanter is buried here: in 1643 Scottish Presbyterians entered into 'the Solemn League and Covenant' to defend Presbyterianism – which recognizes no prelates (bishops or other clergy of exalted rank). Many died for their faith. Part of the inscription runs:

Here lyes Daniel McMichael shot dead at Dalveen by Sir John Dalziel

for his adhering to the Word of God, Christ's kingly government of His House and the Covenanted work of Reformation against tyranny, perjury and prelacy 1685.

About 20 miles (32 km) north of Dumfries, to the east of the A76, off the A702 (map page 58)

East Harling's fine Perpendicular church

Continued from page 82

This spire is unusual – short, lean and lead-covered, it is set at the centre of the tower top, and supported by eight miniature flying buttresses. The battlements and pinnacles of the tower are also highly elaborate.

The glass of the east window was given to the church by Sir Robert Wingfield in 1480 and remains largely as it was then. To escape destruction by Cromwell's men, it was hidden in the attics of the manor house (now gone), where it remained until rediscovered in 1736. Removed again for safety in World War II, when East Anglia was threatened by German sorties against the fighter and bomber bases, the glass was put back in place in 1947.

Medieval window glass tended to be translucent rather than transparent, and seems to cast a warm light. Among the various panels showing scenes from the life and Passion of Christ is one (on the bottom row) showing the donor,

and another depicting Sir Robert Chamberlain. Both were husbands of Anne Harling, who was largely responsible for financing the Perpendicular parts of the church.

There are two memorial helmets, beside the east window, and some fine tombs; in the Lady Chapel at the end of the south aisle is an effigy of a man with his feet resting on a bundle of peacock feathers. His wife's feet lie on what at first sight looks like arms holding a scalp, but is in fact a Saracen's head! These were the family's armorial crests.

8 miles (13 km) north-east of Thetford,
on the B1111, 2 miles (3 km) south of
the A11 (map page 57)

◆

EATON BRAY BEDFORDSHIRE
ST MARY THE VIRGIN

As is often the case, this church was partly rebuilt and enlarged during the 15th century, with Perpendicular windows replacing older ones. The roof was also raised and clerestory windows inserted. The outside is mainly 15th-century, but the western tower was completely restored early in the 20th century.

The entrance door, on the south side of the church, is a masterpiece of scrolled ironwork, from the hand of a master blacksmith some 700 years ago. By 1900, the original door was so decrepit that the ironwork was removed in four pieces and refitted on to new wood.

The Perpendicular features of the exterior are misleading, for the interior is a beautiful example of the first pure Gothic style – Early English – with its strong definition. On the mid 13th-century north arcade of the nave the pillars are made up of eight shafts. Above the shaft rings these become the stalks of the deeply cut foliage of the capitals (each slightly different) from which spring the deep roll mouldings of the arches. Truncated arches also spring from above the capitals at right angles to the arcade, towards the north wall, where corresponding arches begin at a very low angle. It is not known if this highly unusual arrangement was ever completed.

The font is roughly contemporary with the north arcade and carries the same stiff-leaf foliage, although it is slightly less formal. The earlier south arcade, built by about 1220 with polygonal pillars, has plainer stiff-leaf foliage and arches.

One quaint feature of the church is easiest to see with binoculars: the 13th-century corbels, which carry the 15th-century roof, are carved with heads which may well represent the villagers of that time. They were repainted in the 1960s.

The two massive oak and iron hooks hanging on the west wall of the nave were to tear burning thatch from cottages.

3 miles (5 km) west of Dunstable,
2 miles (3 km) north of the B489
(map page 57)

Stiff-leaf carving on the font at Eaton Bray

EDINGTON WILTSHIRE
ST MARY, ST KATHARINE AND ALL SAINTS

This is a historic parish, for from the downs above the church rushed the forces of Alfred the Great in AD 878 to defeat the Danes so decisively at the Battle of Edington.

This collegiate church has a nave with clerestories, aisles to each side, a central tower with transepts to north and south and a long chancel (a third of the whole length). As usual in a monastic-style church, this was the choir for the brothers – there were 18 of them in 1382. The chancel has richly carved detail, such as the paired niches between the fine windows, in which two of the original statues remain. In contrast to the 'private' areas, the nave – which was the parish preserve – is much plainer with small, simple windows. Only at the west end is there some display, with a large window of eight lights. Edington is one of few such churches which have survived more or less intact – often only the nave remains from the former monastic building.

Built between 1352 and 1361, it was one of the very first buildings to show new Perpendicular features among the older Decorated style. In the east window, for example, the two centre mullions ignore the Decorated tracery and rise straight to the arch in fairly typical Perpendicular fashion. The aisle windows do not have this novel feature. The west window, however, is entirely Perpendicular.

There are some splendid effigies and tombs; the Lewis tomb on the south side of the chancel has 'weepers' – the couple's five children, accompanied by a pair of angels.

Some of the original glass remains in the north transept. Also of interest are the 21 remaining consecration crosses. These usually disappeared during the Reformation. At about 8 ft (2.5 m) above the ground, 12 were placed inside and 12 outside when the church was consecrated, to guard against the devil. Some of those inside have been refilled with brass.

4 miles (6.5 km) east of Westbury, on
the B3098 (map page 57)

ESCOMB COUNTY DURHAM
ST JOHN THE EVANGELIST

This small 7th-century Saxon church has the tall, lean look of early Celtic churches. It is a two-celled building with a simple, aisleless nave, leading through a narrow

The 14th-century church at Edington contains a mixture of Decorated and Perpendicular styles

round-arched gap to a narrower, square-ended chancel or sanctuary. Except for some windows, it has remained almost unaltered. Even its roof timbering is ancient, and some of it may be Saxon.

The square-cut stones at the top of the walls were probably pillaged from the Roman fort at nearby Binchester; the wall bases have much bigger stonework. There is typical Saxon long-and-short work at the corners. The small Saxon windows remain, those on the north wall with unusual flat lintels at the top, those elsewhere with rounded lintels hollowed out from one stone.

Other Saxon features include the cross behind the altar, which may be the preaching cross that predated the church, and there are fragments of other crosses in the porch. The roughly circular area of the churchyard shows that this was probably a Celtic churchyard. The small sundial on the south wall is probably Saxon; above the fan of three scratched lines giving the times of services is a crown above a serpent – the latter being a symbol of a god worshipped by the Angles, whose territory this was. It is an example of the young Christian Church adopting earlier symbolism.

Other, later, symbolism can be seen on two gravestones near the porch, each with a carved skull and crossbones. This has nothing to do with pirates, but represented what was thought to be the minimum from which a body could be resurrected on Judgement Day.

A second, early 17th-century sundial on the porch has roman numerals, as it predates the time when arabic numerals came into general use.

1 mile (1.5 km) west of Bishop
Auckland, off the B6282 (map page 58)

◆

EWELME OXFORDSHIRE
St Mary

The church, almshouses and school of Ewelme form a delightful late medieval group. Apart from the 14th-century tower, the battlemented church is much as it was when finished in around 1450, a fine example of late Perpen-

Escomb's fine Saxon church

dicular architecture. Its walls are a patchwork of brick, stone and flint. Inside, there have been few changes – the rood has gone, but the contemporary font and its 10 ft (3 m) high wooden cover remain. The pulpit dates from the 1830s, when the present pews were also installed (an original oak bench remains in St John's Chapel, to the south of the chancel).

This chapel has a painted roof, with carved angels and shields carrying the monogram IHS (a short form of the Greek *Iesous*), which also patterns the walls here. The chapel is a treasure-house of heraldry. Its east window has fragments of the original stained glass, depicting coats of arms; the original tiles around the altar (which are now in the chancel) carry a heraldic fork-tailed lion; the two tombs are also adorned with coats of arms and other heraldic symbols, especially the Chaucer tomb (of the poet's son and his wife). The other tomb, standing between the chapel and the chancel (not its original position), is of their daughter Alice, Duchess of Suffolk, and dates from about 1475.

The walls at Ewelme are a distinctive patchwork of brick, stone and flint

The tomb is a masterpiece of medieval art. Beneath an elegant and intricate canopy, which is surmounted by carved wooden figures – among the earliest extant examples in Britain – is the alabaster effigy of Alice, lying as if asleep, hands clasped in prayer. The canopy (carved from a single block of alabaster) and effigy rest on a tomb chest, which is guarded by knights and others bearing heraldic shields, and in which her remains still lie. There are always fresh flowers in the bowl at her feet.

Below this tomb chest is an open space, within which lies the figure of death – a decaying corpse shrunken in its shroud. The ceiling of this compartment is painted, although this can only be seen by someone kneeling on the floor!

Other memorials and brasses, from all periods, make this a memorable church. The gravestone of the author Jerome K. Jerome is in the churchyard.

13 miles (21 km) south-east of Oxford,
1 mile (1.5 km) off the B4009, east of the
A423 (map page 57)

◆

FAIRFORD GLOUCESTERSHIRE
St Mary

Nobly set in its churchyard, this complete Perpendicular church was consecrated in 1497, replacing an older building. It is more or less rectangular in plan, with a magnificent central tower and porch. As is often the case, the rebuilding was largely due to one man, in this case John Tame, who became prosperous from the wool trade. It was finished by his son, and both are buried and commemorated with brasses within the church.

An insight into the imagination of those times is given by the glass in the windows. No other parish church in Britain has kept a complete set of medieval glass – if not destroyed at the Reformation, it usually fell to Puritan zealots.

There are 28 complete windows, including those in the clerestory, amounting to over 2000 square feet of glass. In

The Perpendicular church at Fairford

days of general illiteracy, they gave a commentary on Christian belief. The series begins (in the north wall opposite the organ) with Eve taking the fruit from the tree in the Garden of Eden; the serpent is blue, and has the head and bust of a woman and the paws of a cat. The following windows (moving eastwards) show the Nativity, the flight into Egypt and other New Testament scenes. Fifth is the great east window over the altar, which shows the events centring on the Crucifixion. The east window in the south aisle shows the tradition, not recorded in the Gospels, that the risen Christ came first to visit his mother, who is seen here leaving her bedroom to greet her son. Elsewhere in this window women wear Tudor dress; perhaps one represents the wife of John Tame.

Subsequent windows and the clerestory show apostles and other saints and martyrs. The west window carries the Last Judgement; below it shows St Michael weighing the worth of a soul while a red devil tries vainly to alter the balance. Below, a blue-bearded devil is shown carting an old man to hell in a wheelbarrow. Satan has a fish's head, and a stomach complete with eyes and sharp teeth. It is worth taking binoculars to see this spectacular series.

The chancel stalls, which are roughly contemporary with

the building, have entertaining misericords, including one that shows a youth teasing a girl and another with a woman belabouring her husband.

8 miles (13 km) east of Cirencester, on
the A417 (map page 57)

---◆---

FARLEY WILTSHIRE
ALL SAINTS

Brick became a popular material for new churches in late Stuart and Georgian times. Most churches built during this period were in cities, but here we have a charming countryside example, its mellow brickwork set off with parapets and other dressings of whitish limestone.

It was built in 1688–90 to a cruciform plan with a western tower, by one of Wren's master masons, and is often mistakenly called a Wren church because of its simple classicism. Wren may well have helped with its design, however. Classical features here include the urns and round-headed windows, most of which have kept their plain glass.

The inside lives up to the promise of the outside, and is equally simple. The font cover, communion table and the 17th-century silver are all original, and the screens were installed in the 18th century. There is a fine set of memorial tombs and funeral hatchments in the Ilchester Chapel.

These last were often the only touch of colour in a Georgian church. However, the church was 'restored' in the late 19th century; a 'Byzantine' reredos was installed, perhaps in place of some original oak panelling, and the sanctuary was tiled (and more tiles added above the panelling that remained). The original box pews were cut down, and the original three-decker pulpit taken away. The present pulpit has carved wooden panels from the Elizabethan period, which may come from an earlier church.

5 miles (8 km) east of Salisbury, 3 miles
(5 km) south of the A30 (map page 57)

---◆---

FELMERSHAM BEDFORDSHIRE
ST MARY

This is a fine Early English church built between 1220 and 1240, with some later work and Victorian restoration. It stands among trees on slightly raised ground and dominates the village buildings scattered down to the river and bridge.

The pride of the church is the west front, with its fine decoration in three stages. Early English dogtooth moulding can be seen in the arcade of seven 'lancets' running across above the doorway. These form a *blind arcade*, only indented into the wall, unusual in that the pillars from which the arches spring are detached from the wall. Above this are two typically Early English lancet windows to each side; in the Perpendicular period the central window probably replaced three original lancets. The roof would have originally been steeply pitched with a gable end (there is evidence of this on the tower). Although it has been lowered and given a Perpendicular parapet, the harmony of the proportions of the west face is not diminished.

There is a sanctuary ring on the old oak door in the south wall, which miscreants could grasp to claim temporary immunity from persecution or prosecution.

A view of the west front at Felmersham

Inside is a world fit for a cathedral, yet this is only a country church. Nave arcades, of circular pillars alternating with octagonal, march majestically to the great compound piers at the crossing which support the central tower. The south transept leading from this crossing is, however, curiously shallow compared with the rest of the building.

The delicate Perpendicular screen dividing the nave from the chancel is 15th-century, and retains its red, gold and blue colouring. In the chancel, the part of the building worst affected by the Victorian restorers, some of the lancet windows are original and pure, while others are imitations. The difference is obvious. The east window is in 'Decorated' style – although the glass dates from the 1950s. The stone pulpit dates from 1875 and was paid for by a subscription of £75.

6 miles (9.5 km) north-west of Bedford,
2 miles (3 km) west of the A6
(map page 57)

◆

GAYHURST BUCKINGHAMSHIRE
ST PETER

One of the finest Georgian churches in the country, St Peter's dates from 1742 to 1748, built to replace one that was 'very old, uncomely and ruinous'. Some think that it is a Wren church, but this is unlikely as he died in 1723. It does, however, owe much to his influence, and forms a noble pair with the somewhat older great house nearby.

There is a good balance in the exterior design, and many architectural touches of elegance: the urns and little cupola which top the broad tower; the bell openings with patterned stone tracery. On the south side a dainty triangular pediment caps two Ionic half-columns. The doorway between these is topped with a bold semicircular pediment. The north side is a witty 'mirror' of this, with the triangle above the door, and the semicircle uniting the half-columns.

Inside, the church remains almost as it was when it was finished. There is fine plasterwork; in the nave ceiling it is restrained, but in the chancel it is more exuberant, with a leaf-motif decoration. The Ten Commandments on the text boards backing the altar start with the old-fashioned double negative: 'Thow shalt not have none other Gods but me'.

Almost everything below the plaster line is oak; the panelling, the box pews and the pulpit. This was once a three-decker, but the lower, clerk's desk has gone. The octagonal, movable font is unusual.

There is a splendid monument to Sir Nathan Wrighte and his son George, their statues standing side by side in full dress and wigs of the time. George Wrighte commissioned this church. The inscription tablet is blank. It is said that George's son, angry at having to pay for the cost of finishing the building and the monument after his father's death, refused to have their names carved.

3 miles (5 km) north-west of Newport
Pagnell, on the B526 (map page 57)

◆

GRASMERE CUMBRIA
ST OSWALD

This church was built mainly in the 14th century and, like many others, is on the site of earlier churches. There is a tradition that St Oswald, a warrior and Christian king of Northumberland, preached here in about AD 640, and it is to him that the church is dedicated.

It is also linked with another giant among men – William Wordsworth, the poet who transformed our feelings for the natural world. He lived nearby, and there is a memorial to him inside the church. He is buried, with Mary his wife, in the churchyard, and the graves of two of their children and his sister Dorothy are nearby.

Wordsworth found poetry in the world around him, capturing it with simple, everyday language. The roof of Grasmere church caught his eye:

> . . . *the roof upheld*
> *By naked rafters intricately crossed,*
> *Like leafless underboughs in some thick wood*
> *All withered in the depth of shade above.*

Continued on page 97

Guided Tour

FRESSINGFIELD SUFFOLK
St Peter and St Paul

The church stands proudly on rising ground at the centre of a pretty village. Suffolk is noted for its fine Perpendicular churches and this is among the best. Increasing wealth gained in the 15th century from dealing in cloth and wool is reflected in Perpendicular additions to an older building; the benches and hammerbeam roof dating from this time are magnificent.

The earliest work such as the west window of the tower is early 14th-century in Decorated style, but the aisles, the clerestory and the south porch are early 15th-century. The south porch was erected around 1420 in memory of a warrior husband and son who fell at Harfleur and Agincourt. It has splendid 'flushwork' – panelling in flint and stone. As was usual at that time, there is heraldic decoration on its front, with family coats of arms, crowns and flowers and two large roses. At the far (eastern) end of the roof nave is a Sanctus bell turret ornately buttressed and decorated and surmounted by a cross. Very few of these survived Puritan destruction.

Inside, the porch roof is vaulted, with carved bosses and corbels. A large central boss depicts the Assumption of the Virgin, while the corbels are carved with the symbols of Matthew, Mark, Luke and John. There is an upper storey (entered from within the church), lit by the small double window above the entrance. Note the fine 15th-century timber doors.

At the entrance is a mat for wiping feet – this church is carpeted throughout. A plain octagonal font and medieval chest (the parish strong-box – with the usual three locks) immediately catch the eye. Arcades with octagonal pillars and moulded capitals divide the nave from the aisles. The east end of the south aisle was a chapel; the ogee-headed piscina (used for washing the sacred vessels) which accompanied the original chapel altar remains. The Decorated tracery of the west window of this south aisle contrasts with the other, Perpendicular, windows.

From the next vantage point, with back to the entrance to the tower (here a door instead of the more usual arch), the full glory of the Perpendicular clerestory is revealed. There are six windows on each side. High in the east end of the nave is another three-light window, as is sometimes found in Perpendicular churches both in East Anglia and in parts of the Cotswolds.

These windows bring light to the single-hammer-beam roof. Although the customary carved angels at the ends of the beams and the figures at the bottom of the wall posts are gone, some good carving remains along the cornice at the top of the nave wall and elsewhere. The north aisle roof is also medieval, with carved corbel heads and carved wheels as decoration.

The chancel also has a medieval roof, its supporting timbering studded with heraldic shields. The arch and supports of the east window are 14th-century, the capitals carved with foliage and heads, but the stone tracery is Victorian. Other

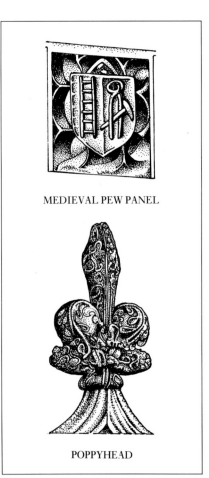

MEDIEVAL PEW PANEL

POPPYHEAD

windows in the chancel contain fragments of the original medieval glass – heraldic shields in the south windows, foliage in the tracery of the north.

Fressingfield is one of Suffolk's finest Perpendicular churches, the profits from wool and cloth paying for radical additions in Perpendicular style

The greatest treasures of this church are its carved benches. They date from 1470 and still stand more or less in their original positions. The ends have carved ornament, with a poppyhead accompanied (where they remain) by human and animal figures. (A full description appears in the church handbook.) The backs of many benches are also decorated, and of greatest interest are the rear benches on each side, known (because of their carv-

ings) as the Passion (north) and Dedication (south) benches. Along the Passion bench, circles with a twisted-spoke design alternate with shields carrying symbols of Christ's Passion – a cock crowing; the nails, cross and crown of thorns; the seamless coat and the dice.

About 10 miles (16 km) east of Diss, on the B1116, 3 miles (5 km) south of the A143 (map page 57)

St Oswald's at Grasmere, built mainly in the 14th century

Continued from page 93

The rather eccentric muddle of timbers is difficult to miss. By 1500 the church was too small, and it was enlarged with a separate aisle to the north, with its own ridged roof. But the valley between the original and new roofs turned out to be a snow trap. So in the 1560s, money was bequeathed for the roof to be 'taken down and maide oop again'. The builder simply added a third roof above the line of the previous ones, but left their timbers in place.

There have been later alterations, to the windows, for example: the east window now contains clear glass, allowing a view of the fells beyond. The Ten Commandments and other creeds are mounted on the walls on framed boards in 18th-century fashion.

An ancient custom is maintained here on St Oswald's Day, 5 August, when the church floor is strewn with rushes, for warmth and (as some were buried under it) freshness. If available, the wild sweet flag, smelling strongly of tangerines, was preferred.

3 miles (5 km) north of Ambleside, on
the A591 (map page 58)

◆

GREAT BOOKHAM   SURREY
St Nicholas

This is a delightful church, with examples of most medieval architectural styles. It is mentioned in the Domesday Survey of 1086, but very little of the 11th-century church remains; there are two windows above the north arcade, one of which has the remains of Norman wall painting from about 1100.

The original church was enlarged twice during the 12th century. In about 1140, the south wall of the nave was demolished, and a south aisle added. Only the arcade remains from this time, and is typically Norman, with massive round pillars, simple scallop capitals and rounded arches. The font (but not its base and stem) is also of this date.

The north aisle was added in about 1180; the wall was pierced through to form the arcade, and its angular pillars, smooth, cushion capitals and pointed arches are typically

Transitional. The tower was also started at this time. Both of the aisles were later altered: the south one in the 14th and 15th centuries, and the north one in the 1840s.

The chancel was altered in the 14th century, and is clearly out of line with the nave. This misalignment is seen in many churches, and some think that it was a deliberate, if obscure, reference to Christ's head falling to one side as he hung from the cross. Cut into the east wall is a very fine 14th-century inscription, recording this rebuilding.

The chancel has a fine set of Decorated windows, although the glass is not original. The east window, a mid 19th-century copy of the original, is renowned for its panels of 15th-century Flemish glass. This graced a French church, from where it was smuggled to England during the French Revolution and used in a Norfolk chapel. When this chapel was closed down, the glass was sold off, and was incorporated into the east window here in 1954. Other panels of the same set can be seen in York Minster.

The stone tower was started at the same time as the north arcade was built (1180). It rises to about the height of the nave walls. Above this are a timber extension and spire, with supporting oak beams five or six centuries old. The wooden shingles of the roof are thicker at one end than the other, and split from the block rather than sawn. They have to be replaced approximately every 70 years; this was last done in 1972.

2 miles (3 km) west of the centre of
Leatherhead, just north of the A246
(map page 57)

◆

GREAT PACKINGTON   WARWICKSHIRE
St James

This unique and interesting church was built from 1789 to 1790. It is square, and its severe classicism gives it a forbidding prison-like face. It has four corner towers with squat, decorative cupolas topped with pinnacles. Only the scatter of gravestones (and the yet-young yew trees) tell you that it is a church.

The classical church of Great Packington

The architect, Joseph Bonomi (1739–1808), was Italian, and many features of this church echo Roman buildings, as well as the ideas of Andrea Palladio. The semicircular windows, for instance, are a fairly common Palladian motif. They are called thermal windows, because they are found on the *thermae*, or baths of Diocletian, in Rome.

Inside, the plan is unusual; it is a *Greek cross* (the four arms are the same length). The corners of the building (underneath the towers) are occupied by separate rooms. The 'arms' are vaulted, and the whole is faced with smooth, painted ashlar. In the eastern arm of the cross is the altar; its communion rail, the surrounds to the reredos, the pulpit and the lectern are all made of white marble and represent an early use of this expensive material. On the other hand, the barriers between the central space and the transepts are made of plaster, and painted to look like wood! In the north transept is the organ, which is said to have delighted Handel and may have been designed by him.

Just east of the A452, about 1 mile
(1.5 km) north of its junction with the
A45 between Coventry and
Birmingham (map page 57)

GREAT WITLEY   HEREFORD AND WORCESTER
St Michael

The great house which this church served is now ruined. The church was consecrated in 1735, but was remodelled inside only 12 years later. Its west end – with two Tuscan columns supporting a pediment, above which is a bell turret tipped by a cupola – reflects the Baroque of Wren and his followers.

Its remodelled interior is a golden and white masterpiece of rococo decoration. The walls and ceilings are decorated in an ornate style which might seem a rather foreign intrusion into an English church. It is foreign in more than one way, for much of the decoration was brought from a grand mansion at Canons Park in what is now north London, which had to be sold off to repay its owner's large gambling debts.

From there came the ten exquisite painted glass windows (which do not look much like traditional stained glass) and, among other things, the three large ceiling paintings. Their vertiginous perspective creates the impression of peering up into the vastness of the sky. They are fitted here with papier mâché frames, which had been moulded from original stucco work at Canons Park. Much of the ornament of this church is in papier mâché, which was then a new concoction.

Rather insensitive to their rococo setting are the Victorian additions of seating and font, the last of which is in Gothic style.

There is an exuberant monument in the transept, a development from the lifelike memorials of the mid 18th century. The effigy is set against a pyramid which is symbolic of immortality. The pensive figures are clothed in classical dress.

10 miles (16 km) north-west of
Worcester, on the A443 (map pages 56–7)

Right *A charming glass window (c. 1719) at Great Witley*

The ancient timber walls at the north-west corner of Greensted church

The church at Greensted, dating from Saxon times

GREENSTED ESSEX
ST ANDREW

This church is not quite what it seems at first glance. Although its 17th-century tower is prettily clad in white Essex weatherboarding and topped by a shingled spire, the nave and chancel look comparatively modern, apparently as a result of drastic Victorian restoration. But closer inspection reveals that the tiled nave roof and the door and windows of the chancel are from about 1500.

These features are all youngsters, however, compared with the real interest of this church. The nave walls are formed of massive split tree trunks, stained by time. They date from around AD 850 and are the only wooden Saxon church walls to remain in Britain. Each giant vertical log originally had a tenon (or tongue) at its base which fitted into a hole or groove in a horizontal wooden beam lying on the ground. The top of each upright was cut away to slot into a grooved beam, secured by wooden pegs of the kind seen fastening the beams of many farmyard barns today. By Victorian times the bottoms of the upright timbers were rotting, so these were shortened and footed on to a brick base.

The original chancel would have been similar. This Saxon building must have been gloomy. There were no windows (the dormer windows were added when the roof was tiled in about 1500), although there were a few 'eye holes'. The darkness would have been relieved with lamps, torches or candles (there are dark patches, perhaps scorch marks, on the south wall).

The ancient baulks of wood are worth close inspection, particularly inside, where they have been smoothed off. There is one original corner log remaining, at the north-west – instead of being split in half, it has had a quarter segment removed. The three flat logs on the north wall block the original doorway.

Humble though such a church would seem, it was still a fairly bold and imposing construction compared with the huts of the villagers it served.

About 12 miles (19 km) west of
Chelmsford, south of the A414
(map page 57)

GRESFORD CLWYD
ALL SAINTS

This is among the finest Perpendicular churches in Wales. There are fragments of 13th- and 14th-century stonework, such as the interior east wall of the tower, but what we see is largely from the late 15th century. It was vast for the size of the village – even in 1589 there were only 20 houses. The source of the money for its rebuilding is unknown. In rich 'wool' areas such as East Anglia and the Cotswolds, small parishes could afford to rebuild extravagantly, but although Gresford was at that time an enormous parish, of 30 square miles (78 square km), it was poor. Perhaps the parish owned some relic or figure that brought pilgrims and their gifts; and which was destroyed at the Reformation.

The upper part of the tower has fairly typical ornament. Some figures escaped destruction at the Reformation – two in niches on the buttresses, for example. The grand south porch is also a typical 16th-century Perpendicular addition; a weather-worn statue of the Virgin survives above the door.

A corner of the impressive Perpendicular church at Gresford

The whole church, with an aisle to either side of the nave continuing into a chapel either side of the chancel, forms the standard Perpendicular rectangle.

The screen between the chancel and nave is finely carved with fan vaulting springing up to its cornice. In the chancel, the two rows of stalls have double-headed finials at either end, and there are quaint depictions on some of the misericords (the hinged seats), one of which shows the devil wheeling sinners to hell. The east window contains some 15th-century glass panels mixed in with Victorian replacements. The Tree of Jesse of the tracery is mostly from about 1500. In the south aisle, there is a Romano-British stone showing one of the Three Fates. Not far away is the stone effigy of a warrior in chain mail – Madoc ap Llewelin, who died in 1331.

4 miles (6.5 km) north of Wrexham, on
the A483 (map page 58)

HADDINGTON LOTHIAN
St Mary

This 14th-century abbey church is the largest parish church in Scotland. It stood for some time partly in ruins, although the nave was always kept as the parish church. The restoration of choir and transepts was completed in 1973, and these restored areas are, unusually, roofed in fibreglass! The communion table is placed at the centre of the crossing of the transepts and nave, with the pulpit and choir seats nearby.

Scotland did not adopt the Perpendicular style of architecture, but developed Decorated into even more flamboyant lines. This development closely echoed that seen in France, with which Scotland then had strong political links. The window tracery displays what is recognized as this Scottish Flamboyant style.

The church is known as the 'Lamp of Lothian', not because of its fine quality, but because the tower was once topped by a lantern. This exterior, as a whole, is worth inspecting; it is decorated and has niches for statuary. The

statues have gone, but some interesting gargoyles remain.

Cassettes and other guides to this popular church are available for visitors, of whom there are usually 12,000 in the summer season.

About 15 miles (24 km) east of
Edinburgh, on the A1 (map page 59)

HALES NORFOLK
St Margaret

This pretty, thatched church stands unused a little way out of today's main village: it is in the care of the Redundant Churches Fund. It is a Norman church of a simple, unchanged plan, with a round western tower, an aisleless nave and an eastern chancel with a rounded (apsidal) end. The only major addition has been that of lancet windows to the nave and to the chancel, where they have been inserted between the original blind arcade. These windows and the east window, with its simple 'Y'-tracery, are from the 13th century. The walls, made of a mixture of materials, including reused Roman tiles, have a lovely texture.

Apart from the windows at the second stage, the flat-topped tower originally presented a blank face; the louvred

The thatched Norman church at Hales

103

openings of the bell chamber and the parapet are later additions. Round towers are quite common in East Anglia; 111 remain in Norfolk, 41 in Suffolk and six in Essex.

Doorways were an important and imposing part of a Norman church: here the north doorway is ornately decorated, with the favourite chevron moulding, stars, and other ornament. The south doorway is also decorated, but is less rich.

The inside walls have retained their plaster, and traces of wall paintings. They are medieval: the elaborate foliage scroll and chevrons over the east window, and the figure of St James in the window splay behind the 18th-century pulpit, are from the 14th century; the St Christopher on the south wall (visible from the north doorway for the benefit of wayfarers) was painted in the 15th century. The majestic octagonal font is from the late 15th century, although the cover was added only in the 17th century. The lower part of the rood screen, painted green and red, remains. A modern touch, which is effective in these surroundings, is the brick support for the altar; this slab of blue lias stone is probably the original for it still carries four consecration crosses, which were usually erased at the Reformation.

About 12 miles (19 km) south-east of
Norwich, on the A146 (map page 57)

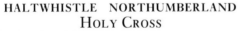

HALTWHISTLE NORTHUMBERLAND
HOLY CROSS

This church, with its churchyard looking out over the Tyne valley, must not be missed. It is a fine example of an Early English building, being all in one style and built in one period in the early 13th century. There has been Victorian restoration, but few would argue with it here. Sash windows had been put in the south aisles and the roof lowered, but the restoration of 1870 replaced these windows with lancets and raised the roof again. The lancet windows of the aisles, clerestory and chancel rank themselves impressively along the rough walls.

The building is spacious; its nave and aisles are broad

and the chancel long. The capitals of the nave arcades are unusual, being irregular octagons from which the arches spring. These are decorated with dogtooth.

Other medieval features include an effigy of a knight, possibly of Thomas Blenkinsopp who died in 1388, grave covers and beautiful three-stalled sedilia in the chancel. These seats for the priest and his helpers are quite unusual, as they are stepped, following the old floor line. The oldest object in the church is a roughly-hewn 7th-century font or stoup displayed in the south aisle. The font in use is 17th-century, but its crude decoration, which might be copied from another source, makes it seem older.

The reredos behind the altar is carved in marble and the rood screen between the nave and the chancel was dedicated in 1923. But the octagonal corbels which carried the old rood beam and the cut marks where it sat against the chancel arch can still be seen. The glass in the east window, a triplet of 15th-century lancets, is probably by the firm of William Morris.

14 miles (22.5 km) west of Hexham, on
the A69 (map page 58)

HIGH HALDEN KENT
ST MARY

This church is renowned for its early 14th-century timberwork. The split halves of a great trunk of oak form the arch of the famous porch, while carved wooden tracery with trefoils, quatrefoils or cinquefoils (three-, four- or five-lobed patterns) decorates the upper part of each side.

The timber tower is even more remarkable. Outside it has a skirt – an octagonal, tiled lean-to – from which rises the square, shingled upper stage. Above this soars the shingled spire topped by a weathercock. Within the tower an intricate cat's-cradle of massive beams can be seen, the main ones thrusting 40 ft (12 m) up from their footing on horizontal sills, and all tied by strengthening trusses. Almost 50 tons of timber were used.

There are a few blocks of imported Caen stone in some

High Halden, famous for its timberwork

of the window-jambs, possibly reused from a Norman building. The lancet window and the remains of the sedilia in the chancel are from the 13th-century extension of this part of the church. The font is a simple, Early English example, a plain square bowl on a large central pillar with the four corners 'supported' by rather slender columns. The parish chest in the chapel south of the chancel may date from the 14th century, like the wooden tower.

As is so often the case, succeeding centuries added here, removed there, destroyed this, and repaired that to make a varied but lovable interior. There is some old glass, including what is thought to be the earliest heraldic quartering (a heraldic shield divided into four sections) in England in the north chancel window. The three arches of the arcade between the nave and south aisle are Perpendicular, 15th-century work, of very high quality.

3 miles (5 km) north-east of Tenterden,
on the A28 (map page 57)

HILLESDEN BUCKINGHAMSHIRE
ALL SAINTS

Hillesden's windows and battlements suggest that it is a superb example of a Perpendicular church. This impression is confirmed by the small turret, with its flying buttresses and pinnacles, above the staircase of the two-storeyed vestry. The porch is elegantly vaulted. The holes in the door are said to be from bullets fired by Oliver Cromwell's household guard when they were besieging Royalists within the church – the wind whistles through them still today.

The promise of the exterior is fulfilled in the pure late 15th-century Perpendicular of the interior. The austere stone-panelled walls, which are unusual in a village church, provide a perfect setting for the elegant arcades. The pews are handsome in their simplicity. The church is very light, for only a few of its large windows bear any stained glass; but one in the south transept has richly coloured scenes of the eight miracles of St Nicholas. Judging by its lively realism it is probably 16th-century Flemish Renaissance work – the stock formal canopies and other backgrounds of earlier glass are replaced by naturalistic landscapes with people looking like real people.

The wooden rood screen has fan vaulting which supports the rood beam. The chancel walls have more decoration than those of the nave and aisles, with panels of tracery, above which a frieze of angels play instruments and carry scrolls.

The chapel to the north of the chancel holds the monument to the Civil War squire who led the resistance to Cromwell's army.

It was this church which inspired the locally-born Sir Gilbert Scott, a leading Victorian architect, with his passion for Gothic. He drew the church when he was 15 years old (the drawing hangs in the vestry), and restored it sensitively when he was 40, to the building we see today.

3 miles (5 km) due south of
Buckingham, reached by a tangle of
country roads (map page 57)

Hillesden – its fine turret, battlements and windows are in the Perpendicular style

HOLME UPON SPALDING MOOR
HUMBERSIDE
ALL SAINTS

Magnificently situated on an isolated hill in the Vale of York, this church is rather far from its village. This could be because it had been an earlier pagan ritual site; or perhaps the earlier settlement migrated from the *holm* or island when the lower marshy ground became dry enough to build on.

A church here was noted in the Domesday Survey, but what we can see is from much later. Three bays of the nave aisle remain from the 13th-century building, but most of the fabric is 15th- and 16th-century Perpendicular. The tower is a fine example of the local Perpendicular style. The geology of the local area is complex, and the use of different kinds of stone reflects this.

It is a good church to potter in, to discover this and that, such as the restored remains of a fine screen between chancel and side chapel which dates from 1460. The west gallery was built in 1767 for the orchestra and choir, which were a source of local pride. A written record shows that early in the 19th century there was a 'big bass fiddle played by Harry Johnstone, and a few smaller instruments, a few singers and the Sunday School children'. There are Elizabethan black-letter texts on the east wall of the chancel. In the churchyard, to the left on entering, is a gravestone to Jane, wife of George Alcock, with the surprising epitaph: 'She was virtuous, but not a loving wife'.

Parish records reveal the fate that overtook many such out-of-the-way churches. A Canon complained in 1903 that: 'the tower was never intended to be used as a coal shed, ash heap, timber yard and general receptacle for rubbish ....' Repairs were put in hand from 1906 to 1911, with the aim of refurbishing 'without tampering in the least with its authenticity or effacing its history'. Whether this has been successful you must judge for yourself.

11 miles (17.5 km) north-east of Goole,
on the A614 (map page 58)

ICKLINGHAM SUFFOLK
ALL SAINTS

This church was unused for many years, because today's village merges two parishes. The benefit is that it escaped the zealous hand of Victorian restorers. It is now in the care of the Redundant Churches Fund.

Beneath the roof thatched traditionally with reeds is a church of Norman origin – there are two small blocked Norman windows in the north wall – but most of the building, including the window tracery, is Decorated.

It is light and uncluttered inside; the walls are plain, and the benches low. Benches may have begun to appear in churches towards the end of the 13th century, but it was some time before they came into general use. This early-looking set is probably 15th-century in date. Some of them have ornamental 'poppyheads' at either end. One explanation for this term is that the word comes from the same root as a ship's poop, for they can be elaborately carved, the fleur-de-lis being a favourite motif.

One chest is of great interest. It is made of slabs of oak bound by elaborate iron scrollwork, and patterned in the same style as the door at EATON BRAY (Bedfordshire). Within these chests were stored the churchwardens' accounts, the church plate, wills, and (after the Reformation) the parish registers of births and deaths. They could also act as a strong-box for cash.

On another, plainer chest nearby some original kneelers are usually displayed. Made from tufts of reeds, they are the ancestors of the familiar stuffed fabric hassocks that we use today.

8 miles (13 km) north-west of Bury St
Edmunds, on the A1101 (map page 57)

IFFLEY OXFORDSHIRE
ST MARY THE VIRGIN

This striking late Norman church (dated to around 1170) has a simple plan of nave and chancel, with a central tower but without transepts. This may have its origins in

The late Norman church of Iffley

the occasional Saxon use, as at BARNACK (Cambridgeshire), of a tower as a nave.

In many Norman churches it is the south door which receives imaginative decoration, and St Mary's is no exception. But the west front is even more elaborate. The overwhelming effect is largely due to the repetitive use of beakhead and chevron right around the doorway. The former is a representation of birds' heads biting a stone roll. The round window and the blind window at the top of the west wall are Victorian additions, the round one replacing one that had been positioned here earlier and walled in. The tower is also ornamented outside, though more simply (the battlements are a later addition).

The church is quite dark inside, dominated visually by the tremendous sculpted arches which support the west and east walls of the tower.

Iffley village is embraced by the
southern outer edge of Oxford's
suburbs and the church is just east of
the A4158 (map page 57)

INGESTRE STAFFORDSHIRE
ST MARY

This church, built in 1676, was almost certainly designed by Sir Christopher Wren, architect of St Paul's Cathedral and many other churches in London. This may be the only country church of his design, although FARLEY (Wiltshire) is often claimed to be one.

While keeping to the basic medieval plan of western tower, aisled nave with clerestory (although the round windows are an innovation) and chancel, this is an early 'classical' church. It is grouped with the great house close by (for which it was built), but as it is lower than the approach road, the effect of the tower, and the west portico and doorway, is diminished.

The distinguished interior is elaborate, and largely unaltered – only the garish Victorian glass in the east window is out of keeping. The arcades between the nave and the aisles have slim compound piers, each consisting of four Tuscan columns topped by classical, squared abacuses from which the generously rounded arches spring. Many of Wren's London churches lost their ceilings in the bombing of World War II; here the plasterwork of the ceiling is a riot of decorative detail, including swags of foliage, flowers, fruit and cherub heads.

The floor of the chancel is paved with black and white marble, which was the fashion in London at the time. The chancel was gradually regaining its former importance, after Puritan fervour had diminished, so the communion table (with twisted legs) is back at the east end, surrounded by communion rails (although matins and evensong could be led from the nave).

The pulpit is finely carved, and the oak screen has Composite pilasters, and swags like those on the ceiling.

4 miles (6.5 km) east of Stafford, off the
A51 (map page 57)

Right *The early 'classical' church at Ingestre*

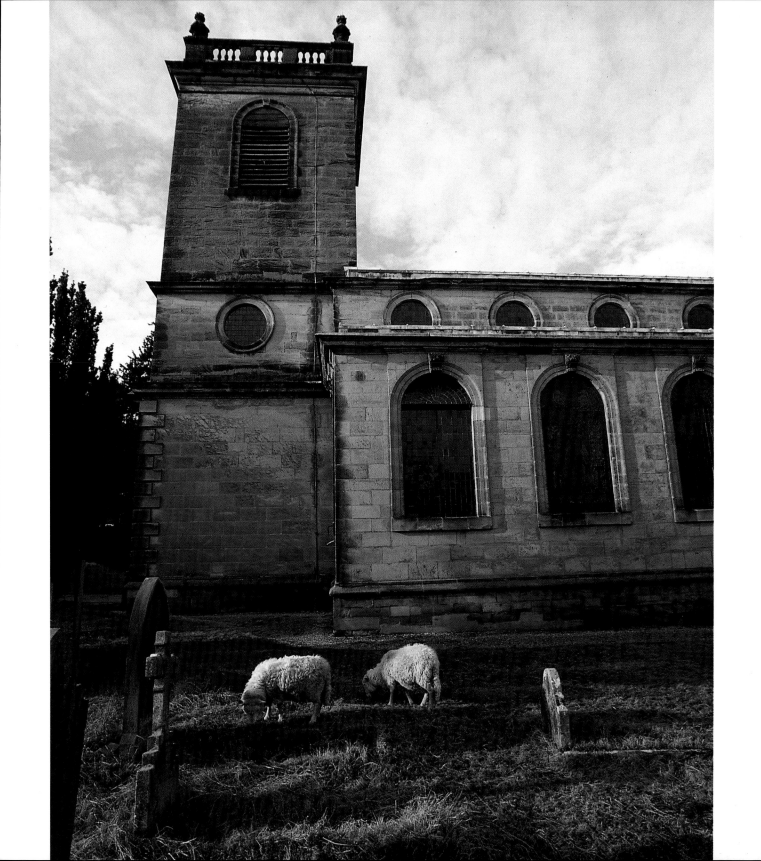

INGLESHAM WILTSHIRE
St John the Baptist

Approached along a narrow track, this church stands with a small scatter of farm buildings. At first glance the trek seems hardly worthwhile, for the plain exterior and the simple bellcote at the west end do not hold out much promise. The bellcote dates from 1270 while the nave, north and south arcades, chancel and south chapel date from around 1200 (the porch is later). The east window, with pointed trefoiled lights, dates from 1290. The aisles were rebuilt with new windows in the 15th century, but the original Transitional arcades remain: the arches are round along the south arcade, and pointed along the north.

In 1888–9 William Morris saved this church from over-zealous restoration, and woodwork fills and spills across the uneven floors. Box pews clutter the nave, encroaching into the aisles. The unrestored medieval screens are a rare sight. The pulpit is lodged in one corner. This homely welcoming jumble is set against walls which are a patchwork of coloured washes and scraps of paintings and texts, including part of the reredos.

One item of note is the late Saxon relief sculpture, perhaps from an earlier church on the same site, set in the wall of the south aisle, showing the Virgin and Child with the Hand of God. The scratch dial, bottom left, suggests that it was originally outside. It is a human piece of work, a rustic cousin to the Christ in Majesty at BARNACK (Cambridgeshire).

7 miles (11 km) north of the edge of
Swindon, off the A361 (map page 57)

◆

ISLE ABBOTS SOMERSET
St Mary

The west tower of Isle Abbots is one of the finest in a county famed for its splendid Perpendicular towers. The bell chamber at top has paired openings and the battlements are pierced, with pinnacles at the corners. Pinnacles also decorate the set-back buttresses (stepped back at each stage). Between the doorway and the bell-chamber openings are three ranks of windows: an unusually large four-light window, a single two-light window, and a pair of two-light windows above. The fame of the church lies in the series of ornate niches still containing statues, which flank the doorway and accompany the windows.

The fan-vaulted porch is also of fine Perpendicular work. There is, unusually, a stoup to the right of the door; as part of the baptism service was held here, it may have served as a font in earlier days. The font in use inside has Norman carvings of dragons, a dove and other symbols.

Below the wagon roof is a simple, satisfying, whitewashed interior. The arches of the north arcade are typically Perpendicular in shape, and as with many churches, the stairs cut into one of the piers, giving access to the rood loft, remain.

The rood screen is rather plain and perhaps came from elsewhere, for this church certainly has pretensions to grandeur. The piscina and sedilia are unique, the former framed by a set of decorated panels with cusped arches, and the sedilia echoing this with shallow blind arcading. They have 'tub' sides – with backs and arms united in a single curve.

Amongst other features of interest are fragments of ruby-red and blue glass in the east window.

7 miles (11 km) south-east of Taunton,
1 mile (1.5 km) off the A378 (map page 56)

◆

KETTON LEICESTERSHIRE
St Mary

This church is famous for its spire, but it has many other grand features. The late 12th-century west front is Transitional: its round Norman doorway is enriched with both the old chevron and the new dogtooth mouldings and flanked by new, blind, Gothic pointed arches.

In the 13th century, aisles were added to the Norman nave with very tall, Early English arches in the arcades, and the Norman arches under the tower were changed from rounded to pointed. The clerestory was inserted in the 15th

Ketton is made up of a mixture of styles

century, and the great west window was reconstructed in the 19th. The Early English lancets of the chancel's north and south walls were also renewed in the 19th century, and lancet windows put in place of the square 17th-century east window. These changes enhance the visual link with the lovely tower and its fine spire.

From its 12th-century roots rises the beautiful 13th-century belfry stage, with a triplet of Early English lancet bell openings on each side; each lancet is further divided into two by a slender column and decorated with the dog-tooth motif.

Above this, the noble 14th-century broach spire rises to 150 feet (46 m). Each of its sloping corner broaches has a decorative figure at the top and further decoration is added by three tiers of openings – for ventilation rather than light or sound. This spire was much admired and imitated in Victorian times.

The tall lancet windows of the chancel lead the eye up to those in the tower, from where it is carried up by the spire itself, crowned with its golden cockerel. The ballflower decoration on the gables of the lowest lights suggests that the spire itself was added later, in the Decorated period, the masons building, literally and metaphorically, on what was already there.

3 miles (5 km) south-west of Stamford,
on the A6121 (map page 57)

KILPECK   HEREFORD AND WORCESTER
ST MARY AND ST DAVID

Although there is a fragment of Saxon masonry, and the name derives from Kil or Cell of St Pedic, which suggests Celtic origins, this is a 12th-century Norman church, with the simple plan of nave, chancel and apsed sanctuary. Only some medieval windows, the bellcote, and such things as the gallery and tomb slabs are later.

Kilpeck is famous for its amazing decoration. From the cold stone, monsters glare and semi-human faces grin. Serpents writhe, lovers clasp, saints stand peacefully, while dog, rabbit and fish peer with expressions that would not be out of place in a modern cartoon.

Many influences come together here. The gargoyle-like heads and other images on the corbels which line the tops of the outside walls might echo the traditions of the Iron Age Celts, who displayed the heads of their slain foes. There is a grotesque breastless female figure showing all, known as a 'sheela-na-gig'. The meaning of these delightful carvings is unclear – only two of the corbels appear to have any Christian significance: they show the Lamb of God.

The south doorway is particularly beautiful. The inter-twining serpents and foliage of the outer door jambs are direct descendants of Viking decoration. On the inner left-hand shaft are two warriors entangled in foliage. Their significance is not understood, but they may be, like those on the chancel arch inside, derived from the church of Santiago da Compostela in Spain, a major pilgrimage church.

The 12th-century Norman church at Kilpeck

Inside the church, the magnificent chancel arch attracts the visitor's attention immediately. The arch is massively, but plainly, ornamented with chevron, but the shafts on each side are intricately carved with more identifiably Christian subjects than is the case outside, such as apostles holding books and emblems – St Peter at the top of the north shaft has a large key. At the foot of this shaft stands a roughly-hewn holy water stoup; the plain font bowl is also Norman but rests on a modern base.

8 miles (13 km) south-west of Hereford,
just to the south of the A465
(map pages 56–7)

◆

KIRKBY MALHAM NORTH YORKSHIRE
ST MICHAEL

More than 10,000 visitors a year come here, and enjoy (as the comments in the visitors' book show) the peace and tranquillity to be found within its walls. Although there was an earlier church, the current building is largely late 15th-century Perpendicular in such things as the tower, windows and battlements to the nave walls. The great rebuilding of about 1490 produced identifiable local characteristics. The tower is an example of the local, rustic 'Craven' Perpendicular, undecorated except for its battlements.

There are many items of interest. Among the oldest is the door in the south porch. It predates the Perpendicular changes and bears a sanctuary ring on its outside. Inside there is an invasion beam to secure it against Scots raiders (churches could be places of refuge at such times). The 11th-century font has an unusual history: it was probably thrown out of the church during the Reformation, and was rescued from a rubbish heap about a century ago and reinstalled.

One unusual architectural feature is that the columns of the main arcades between nave and aisles have decorative niches which (until the Reformation) would have held statuettes of saints. The fine doors of some of the box pews are of interest. Apart from four late 19th-century additions, most of the pews are late 15th- or early 16th-century, many bearing initials of families who used them or (in post-Reformation days) rented them. As weekly attendance at church was then mandatory, the pews raised a considerable revenue. The chest in front of the west screen, dated to the 14th or 15th century, might have continued in use as a strong-box. Typically, it has to be opened with three keys, held separately by the vicar and churchwardens.

The church also contains rather more modern features of interest, including the east window of the chancel, which dates from 1957.

8 miles (13 km) north-west of Skipton,
north of the A65 (map page 58)

◆

LASTINGHAM NORTH YORKSHIRE
ST MARY

This church has an important place in the story of the development of Christianity in Britain. The Venerable Bede, who completed his *History of the English Church and People* in AD 731, tells its story. In the 7th century, Bishop Aidan came to Northumbria from Iona at the invitation of King Oswald. He had founded a school and monastery on the island of Lindisfarne, and among the early pupils were four brothers, all of whom became priests. Two of them, Cedd and Chad, became bishops, and were later venerated as saints. Early in his priesthood, Cedd preached to Northumbria's arch-enemies, the Mercians of the Midlands, and later went as missionary to East Anglia, where he founded monasteries and built churches – that at Bradwell still survives, lonely amongst the marshes of the Essex coast.

However, Cedd's most famous monastery was at Lastingham, which he founded in AD 659, cleansing the site for God by prayer and fasting. It was ransacked by the Danes, but perhaps never deserted. In 1078 Abbot Stephen of Whitby began to rebuild it, creating a crypt where St Cedd's shrine had stood. This crypt remains today, as a church in itself with side aisles and rounded apse circling

The church of St Mary at Lastingham, first founded in AD 659

the altar, to the right of which the body of the saint (who died in AD 664) may lie.

With its weighty arches and early groin vaulting, this crypt has remained virtually unchanged since Norman times. It is also of interest for the carved stones stored here, some of which are parts of churchyard crosses, while others are Viking.

The church above the crypt is also Norman in origin, restored in the 1870s (the brick-vaulted roof was completed in 1879) but with choir stalls and other Victorian trappings. It is the rump of a large church whose nave was never completed; the great pillars at its west end were meant to be supports for a central tower.

About 7 miles (11 km) north-west of
Pickering, north of the A170 (map page 58)

LAUNCELLS CORNWALL
St Swithun

The interior of this church is charming – it is about the only Cornish church to escape Victorian restoration and improvement. Architecturally it is a fairly standard, 15th-century building, the aisles matching the nave in height, with panelled wagon roofs. There is an interesting if slight contrast between the two nave arcades – that to the north is in granite, while that to the south is in local polyphant stone. The capitals have fleur-de-lis patterns which are repeated in the 15th-century tiles in the chancel. These are typical 'encaustic' tiles; such tiles first appeared in the 12th century, and were standard church tiles in medieval times. They were made by impressing the surface with a patterned wooden block, and filling the hollows produced usually with white liquid clay slip, producing (when fired) a white pattern on buff background.

The Norman cable-mounted font is from the earlier church on the same site; it has a 17th-century cover.

Unlike INGLESHAM (Wiltshire), the atmosphere comes not from a homely clutter but from having sufficient space to see details. There are fine old box pews in the north aisle,

and late medieval 16th-century benches with fascinating bench ends. Some have depictions of nails, ladders and other symbols of the Passion, Ascension and Resurrection – which were popular topics in early sets of benches.

The splendid Royal Arms of Charles I on the north wall, of carved and painted plaster, are also noteworthy.

2 miles (3 km) inland from Bude, on
the A3072 (map page 56).

LAVENHAM SUFFOLK
St Peter and St Paul

This is one of the most splendid of the 15th-century 'wool' churches in East Anglia, rebuilt with wealth accruing from the international trade in wool and cloth in late medieval times. It dominates the village streets of half-timbered houses.

Apart from the tall tower of *knapped* (broken) flints with stone cornerings, the church seems all window. This is the wizardry of late Perpendicular style.

The evolution of the church is interesting. The chancel belongs to an older building, with a Decorated east window

The East Anglian 'wool' church of Lavenham

(the brightly coloured glass is Victorian). The 14th-century font also predates its surroundings. Somehow the chancel screen, also from the 14th century, survived not only the rebuilding but the Reformation as well. Some of the misericords of the old chancel stalls express the medieval sense of humour.

The money to pay for such rebuilding might come from two sources: the local aristocracy or the new merchant class. In this case the aristocrat was one of the De Vere family who had been Captain General to Henry Tudor when he won the crown at the Battle of Bosworth Field in 1485, bringing an end to the murderous Wars of the Roses. Perhaps in thanksgiving, De Vere put the work in hand; the beautiful south porch is a personal gift – the shields and boars relate to the family. Lavenham's other main patron came from the steadily growing merchant class; he was Thomas Spryng, known as 'The Rich Clothier'. The church contains a fine Spryng parclose (the relevant will reads: '. . . to be buried in the church of Lavenh'm be fore the Awter of Saint Kateryn where I will be made a Tombe with a Parclose threabout . . .'). In this screened enclosure masses were said for the soul of the dead donor. In addition, south of the chancel there is a Spryng chapel. Thomas also left enough money to finance 'the fynishing of the stepul'.

The bells are famous: the tenor bell which weighs nearly a ton-and-a-half is considered the finest toned bell in Britain, perhaps the world. It was cast in 1625.

On the A1141, 5 miles (8 km) north-east
of Sudbury (map page 57)

◆

LITTLE MAPLESTEAD ESSEX
St John the Baptist

This small building illustrates an intriguing byway in church history. The original church here was built by the Knights Hospitallers (the Knights of St John of Jerusalem), who with the Knights Templars were the most important of the Military Orders of Knighthood. They originated in Norman times, protecting and providing the needs of pilgrims, and played an important role during the Crusades of the 11th, 12th and 13th centuries. The round-naved church plan they adopted was modelled on the Church of the Holy Sepulchre in Jerusalem.

St John's was rebuilt in about 1335 to the older plan, and only this and the Temple (Templars') church in London remain in use, although others are known – in Ludlow Castle, for example. (The 12th-century round-naved churches at Cambridge and Northampton are parish-church copies of the design.)

Long gone is the monastery-like building of the 'hospital' or hospice; it would have been staffed by two or three knights with chaplains, officials and servants. At the Dissolution of the Monasteries, the knights retired to Malta (and became known as the Knights of Malta). The order was revived in the 19th century, undertaking Red Cross and hospital work, such as that of the St John Ambulance Association.

The 14th-century western doorway opens into the six-sided nave, which is only 10 ft (3 m) in diameter, and is surrounded by a circular aisle. To the east is a chancel ending

Little Maplestead, a Crusader church

in a curved apse; in the original this would have been blocked off from the nave with a solid wooden screen and reserved for the knights' own services. There was presumably a second altar for the pilgrims' benefit in the nave.

The oldest remaining item in the church is the roughly carved font. It has a deep bowl, for baptism by complete immersion was the custom in early Norman times.

2 miles (3 km) north of Halstead, to the
west of the A131 (map page 57)

◆

LLANFILO POWYS
ST BILO

With its simple plan and massive nave walls, this church retains its Norman feeling, although the whitewashed walls are likely to have been coloured and patterned then, for the Normans loved decoration for its own sake. There is a blocked-up door in the north wall of the nave, with a Norman ornamented lintel, and the remains of the corresponding lintel to the south door are in the south porch. The original altar slab was found under the chancel floor early this century, where it may have been hidden at the time of the Reformation. The font is probably older, and Celtic; it is too small for the total immersion of the infant which was the custom in Norman days.

There is also some work of Early English date – the cross slab in the sanctuary for example: the flowers carved on either side of the cross may represent those scattered at the time of burial. From the Perpendicular period come the 15th-century oak-ribbed wagon roof – its panels painted white – and the Angelus bell, which now stands on the chancel floor. Its Latin inscription, decorated with the heads of Edward III and Queen Philippa, reads: *Missi de celis habeo nomen Gabrielis* – 'I have the name of Gabriel sent from heaven'.

The rood screen and loft are the pride of the church. Dating from around 1500, they were carefully restored in the 1920s. Bands of intricate lacy carving (characteristic of parts of Wales) adorn them. Above stands a replace-ment rood, and its attendant figures of the Virgin and St John the Baptist.

7 miles (11 km) north-east of Brecon,
south of the A470 (map page 56)

◆

LONG SUTTON LINCOLNSHIRE
ST MARY

The most striking feature of this church is the tower, only just attached to the south-west corner of the south aisle. Although detached towers are generally rather rare, this is not the only one in the area. Presumably, the masons had to look out for the firmest possible ground in this unstable, marshy countryside and suit the shape of the building to the land available.

The buttressed tower is rather Norman in appearance, but the arcade of lancets and the bell openings above are clues to its Early English, 13th-century date. The timbered and herring-boned lead-clad spire is thought to be contemporary with the tower, and if this is so it is one of the earliest in Britain. The *spirelets* (little spires) over the corner-turrets, also of lead-covered timbering, have been likened to candle snuffers in shape.

The Perpendicular south porch, two-storeyed and enriched with battlements and stepped buttresses, is also impressive, if less unusual. Battlements also line the top of the nave wall: their form of 'stepping' is usually restricted to East Anglia.

Inside, the stately Norman nave arcade has massive round-headed arches: the piers are in alternating pairs – two round, two octagonal, and two round.

The churchyard is quite large, and contains many fine Georgian headstones. Such memorials are always worth inspecting, for they can sometimes carry exquisite and distinctive lettering, the work of a local carver.

8 miles (13 km) north of Wisbech, on
the A17 (map page 57)

◆

Guided Tour

◆

MELBOURNE DERBYSHIRE
St Michael with St Mary

This is one of the most magnificent Norman churches in Britain, set in a tree-shaded close on the edge of this small town. The church with its three towers was almost a miniature cathedral in its time, and was built (or rebuilt) in unimportant Melbourne for the use of the Bishop of Carlisle – in case marauding Scots crossed the border and forced him to flee. It proved a necessary refuge — Bishop Adelulf arrived from Carlisle in the mid 12th century.

The view from the close reveals drastic changes to the east end. The chancel has been lowered to a single storey and the weatherline of its original steeply-pitched roof can be seen on the tower. As well as being reduced to one storey, the chancel had its semicircular (*apsed*) end removed in the 16th or 17th century. The line of the blocked-up arch on the south transept illustrates that this (and the north transept) originally ended in apses, too. The flat east ends are pierced with Gothic (Decorated in the south transept, Perpendicular in the chancel) windows, while the side walls of the chancel retain their original Norman ones.

The exterior walls carry many areas of patching with new stone. There has been heavy weathering, particularly obvious on the fortress-like west front of the church, with its two squat towers. It is largely plain except for the heavy chevron and carved capitals of the central doorway. Facing it is a massive Norman tithe barn, its large size perhaps indicating an unusually heavy burden of tithes.

Entrance is by the south door, which has some renewed Norman carving: to the left (behind the west front) is an impressive narthex, a three-bay porch, with a roughly-built groin vault carried on high by thrusting ranks of plain columns. The size of this narthex is one indication of how important this church was: it would have been needed for ceremonials led by the Bishop. Here, too, the unbaptized could follow the service.

A beautifully simple Norman font stands at the junction of narthex and nave. From here, massive round piers (4 ft in diameter) march down the nave to the massive arch at the east end, which is surmounted by a triplet of smaller arches, the central one containing a (modern) rood. The squarish bases of the piers have a kind of 'claw' at each corner, but their meaning is unknown. These piers are so closely set that the arches they bear have had to be stilted to give the required height – that is, they run vertically before turning. The round arches are finely ornamented with chevrons, and there is some carving on the capitals.

The clerestory above these arcades is worth a long look. It has a walkway (*ambulatory*) between the nave windows and clerestory arches; originally this continued around the chancel (before the chancel's height was reduced). Along the north arcade, triplets of round arches lead through to single round-headed windows, all Norman work. On the south, however, the original was replaced in the 13th century with paired, pointed arches opening to pointed windows. The tie-beam roof is

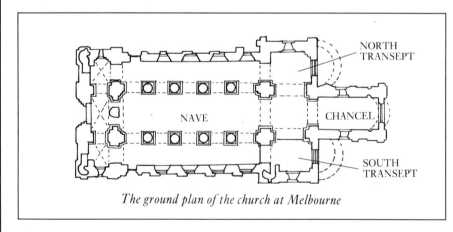

NORTH TRANSEPT

NAVE

CHANCEL

SOUTH TRANSEPT

The ground plan of the church at Melbourne

19th-century (the external weatherlines on the central tower [noted earlier] show that the original was steeper).

Below the main tower, a space now holding the choir and from where the bells are rung, we have a powerful sense of Norman energy. Supported on four powerful rounded arches, the walls above are broken by three sets of three rounded arches, the lowest being a continuation of the clerestory walkway. The upper part of the tower was rebuilt in the 17th century, when the belfry was added. This tower was probably originally vaulted to match the strong architecture of the narthex.

Vivid carving enlivens the capitals of the chancel arch; faces, foliage, a grinning cat and dog and other grotesques are seen here. Opposite, on the north-west tower pillar, are more carvings. Alongside are the remains of a wall painting – showing the devil standing on the backs of two women, perhaps illustrating the sin of idle gossip. It gives a hint of the church's once colourful interior, which would have been covered in paintings such as this – designed to educate, and instil the fear of God in the congregation, in the days when very few could read.

About 7 miles (11 km) south of Derby, on the B587 (map page 57)

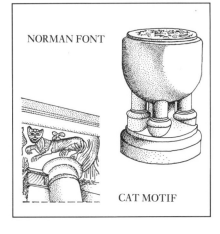

NORMAN FONT

CAT MOTIF

The 17th-century belfry heightens the squat Norman tower of the church at Melbourne

The half-timbered church at Lower Peover

LOWER PEOVER CHESHIRE
ST OSWALD

Cheshire is a black and white county. It was once heavily wooded and without good stone, so many surviving houses and cottages are half-timbered, the infilling plastered and whitewashed.

Few half-timbered churches have survived beetles, accidents of fire and unsympathetic restoration. This is one example, although the exterior is much restored. The west tower is thought to have been erected in the 16th century, but the rest is largely from the 13th century. The oldest wooden object is probably the 13th-century chest hewn out of a single log. The nave has retained its massive roof timbers. Originally, one roof covered the nave and the aisles, separated from each other by octagonal pillars.

The wooden furnishings – altar and rails, screens, and font cover – are mostly Jacobean, and add a richness to the rather dark interior of the church. Some of the box pews have fixed lower door sections. Originally a thick bed of rushes was piled in, to provide some insulation and warmth during winter services.

12 miles (19 km) west of Macclesfield,
on the B5081 to the west of the A50
(map pages 57–8)

MILDENHALL SUFFOLK
ST MARY AND ST ANDREW

This is a fine Suffolk wool church, and an interesting contrast to that at LAVENHAM (Suffolk). Although most of the church dates from the great 15th-century rebuilding, older fabric does remain. The chancel is dated to the 13th century. The vestry to the north of the chancel was originally a separate chapel.

One quirk of this church is that the main entrance has always been to the north; usually it is to the south. The two-storeyed north porch here is long and large, and ornamented and vaulted. (A boy dressed as an angel is said to have stood on the first-floor gallery while the Palm Sunday procession passed beneath.) The south porch is modest in comparison. The great west tower, a typical 15th-century Perpendicular addition, is 120 ft (37 m) high.

Inside, two things catch the eye. The first is the east window, seen through the beautiful Early English chancel arch. Probably of around 1300 in date, its unusual design consists of seven lights and tracery, surrounded by a band which breaks into a border of quatrefoils where it curves. It could probably be classed as Decorated, but is unique.

The second feature is the magnificent roofing, which is a superb example of the local carpentry, and underlines the reputation of English wooden roofs of this time as being second to none. In the nave, tie-beams alternate with hammer-beams (see illustration on page 40). The former are generously decorated with carving, while the latter end in huge carved angels with spreading wings to create one of the region's famous 'angel roofs'. The hammer-beam roofs of the aisles are beautifully carved, especially in the north aisle, with figures of people, angels and monsters, as well as biblical scenes.

The roofs have been restored, and the repairers found that the woodwork was pitted with buckshot, from the time when the Puritans shot down the original angels.

About 9 miles (14.5 km) north-east of
Newmarket, on the A1101 (map page 57)

MINSTEAD HAMPSHIRE
ALL SAINTS

This village can only be approached through unbroken stretches of the New Forest. Seen from the lych gate (which still has its coffin-rest) the church seems indeed a backwoods place, a higgledy-piggledy arrangement of windows and irregular dormers. In fact, if it were not for the 18th-century brick west tower and the tell-tale porch, it would not look much like a church at all. It is one of the select number of churches to escape over-zealous Victorian restoration and it keeps its rustic charm and – more or less intact – the kind of interior which evolved after the Reformation.

Minstead is at heart medieval; entry is by a medieval door in a 12th-century doorway. Like MILDENHALL (Suffolk) the north doorway serves as the main entrance. Inside, the 13th-century chancel arch is skewed by subsidence and time. But the furniture is not the 'Gothic' that the Victorians so often imposed. On either side of the communion table with its communion rails are boards carrying the Ten Commandments. There is a 17th-century three-decker pulpit (the parish clerk led the amens from the bottom rank; the vicar read the scriptures from the middle tier and delivered his sermon from the top level). This pulpit faces rows of 17th-century pews.

The medieval church at Minstead

At the west end of the church are two galleries: the lower is a post-Restoration design, and the upper was for a choir of children from the local charity school. Victorian restorers moved the choir down to the chancel. There also remains a pair of private pews, one of which is entered from the chancel (the private entrance has been sealed off) and has comfortable cushioned seats and a fireplace!

A growing congregation meant that in 1790 an extension was built to the south of the nave; here again are rows of fine old seating that the ecclesiological Victorians despised. The roof beam is shored up by a cast-iron pillar, one of the first to be made. Not far from this pillar stands another clue to the building's real age – a font with crude but dramatic carvings (note the two lions with a shared head) of Norman style.

Sir Arthur Conan Doyle, creator of Sherlock Holmes, is buried in the churchyard.

About 10 miles (16 km) west of
Southampton, just south of the A31
(map page 57)

◆

MONTGOMERY POWYS
ST NICHOLAS

The original building may be 13th-century, but it has later windows and other features (the tower was rebuilt in 1816). The nave has a two-part roof: to the west is a fine open hammer-beam construction, whereas that of the eastern half is a panelled wagon roof, the oak ribs having coloured bosses. This panelling does not hide a continuation of the hammer-beaming, but rather a plain construction.

A double screen separates nave and chancel. The western side belongs to the church, the other most probably came from a priory church at the time of the Dissolution of the Monasteries, together with the stalls. They are all of 15th-century date.

In the south transept is a splendid canopied Elizabethan tomb of 1596, the man shown in full armour, with his wife in an embroidered dress. Behind them kneel their eight

children, while below, as a reminder of the true face of death (for these figures are but resting), is a shrouded corpse. Like other monuments of the time, it is awash with heraldic symbols. There are also medieval effigies on the floor of the transept, showing older armour.

Most visitors make their way to the robber's grave in the churchyard, about 8 yards (7 m) west of the path from the north gate to the tower, and about 12 yards (11 m) from the gate. Here lies John Davies who, in 1821, was publicly hanged in the town for robbing a traveller of a watch worth 30 shillings – in those days a capital offence. To the last he proclaimed his innocence, and prayed that God would not allow the grass to grow over his grave in proof of it. A visit to his grave will show whether or not his prayer has been answered.

7 miles (11 km) directly south of
Welshpool, on the B4388 (map page 56)

NORTHLEACH GLOUCESTERSHIRE
ST PETER AND ST PAUL

This is a fine example of a Cotswold wool church – a wool church being one that was largely rebuilt in the then current Perpendicular style by the clothiers and wool merchants who earned huge fortunes through trade with Europe in the late 14th and 15th centuries. Here the local sheep are the famous Cotswold breed which gave their name to the area. Indeed the memorial brass of one benefactor in this church shows him with his feet firmly on one of the animals (see page 27)!

The western tower of 1350 has panelled battlements, but lacks the pinnacles which were commonly added in this area – perhaps a spire was intended to cap it.

The south porch (1480) with its ogee-headed door and sculpture of the Virgin is one of the finest in Britain. It has two storeys (the fireplace in the upper floor, which was once used as a schoolroom, has a chimney cleverly concealed in

Left The 13th-century church of St Nicholas, Montgomery

one of the crocketed pinnacles). The nave has magnificent lofty arcades, its columns octagonal, with fluted (cut-away) sides, and carrying low, four-centred arches. The 'wineglass'-stemmed stone pulpit, with its carved panels, is a beautiful piece of 15th-century stonework. Another feature is the large window over the chancel arch, similar to others found in churches in Cirencester and other places nearby. They are called 'Cotswold windows'. The roof is rather restrained, lacking the colour and overall carving of East Anglian wool churches.

In 1964 an ironwork screen was erected to separate nave and chancel. There is a nave altar of the same date, but the chancel does now have its original pre-Reformation high altar, a long slab of stone, which was discovered beneath the floor in 1884.

10 miles (16 km) north-east of
Cirencester, just off the A429
(map page 57)

PENMON GWYNEDD
ST SEIRIOL OR ST CYNLAS

Two saints can claim the dedication of this church, for it was founded by St Cynlas who handed it on to his brother St Seiriol in the 6th century. It is in a splendid position looking across the approach to the Menai Strait. It was for many centuries part of a priory complex, of which the prior's house and refectory remain. There is a holy well nearby and what remains of a hermitage beneath a cliff.

Although founded in the 6th century, it was often raided, and the rather small church we see today dates mostly from 1120–70. It is a cruciform building, with a low central tower, capped with its original squat pyramidal roof.

Other Norman features of interest are the south doorway with a weathered dragon occupying the *tympanum*, the space between the curve of the arch and the straight top of the door. Originally a beast of good omen, dragons at some time acquired an evil character – hence the story of St George and the Dragon.

Continued on page 127

Guided Tour

The majestic Decorated church at Patrington is perfectly proportioned and balanced

PATRINGTON HUMBERSIDE
St Patrick

In Sir John Betjeman's words, this church 'sails like a galleon of stone over the wide, flat expanse of Holderness'. It is one of the greatest churches in England; many hold it to be the most beautiful of all. The first close view, from the lych gate alongside the churchyard, supports this claim. Nave and chancel, the aisles and the lovely spire which pierces the vast sky are all in perfect proportion and balance.

It was built over a short span of years, between 1320 and 1349, and is almost entirely Decorated in style, although a Perpendicular east window in the chancel dates from 1410. And it is exuberantly Decorated. Note, for example, the alternating tracery of the windows, down each side of the chancel. The octagonal spire rises from a dainty eight-sided *corona* – a tall crown-like collar made of open panels – with flying buttresses at each corner.

Entry is by the north porch. The carved supports of the arches are typically Decorated. Note the mason's mark containing the letter 'A', incised in many places in this porch. The base of the first pier (pillar) is puzzling; it is much greater in size than the pier it now carries, and presumably remains from an earlier church here. The font is of interest, with 12 delicately carved panels; it looks rather like an elaborate wedding cake.

The south porch is grander than the north and it was the one in main use in the past, as was usual. Above it is a small room, used at various times for parish meetings and as a store room for parish records. Now a chapel, it can be reached from within the church by a narrow staircase beside the south doorway.

The south aisle has some very faint patches of colour, the last relic of wall paintings and painted decoration which would have covered much of the inside walls. Two tombs of clerics rest in the south aisle, the stone slabs incised with crosses of unusual design. The church is notable for its host of carved faces of kings, queens and lesser folk, and of animals real and imaginary. Some lively ones can be seen here, decorating the corbels of the supports for the vaulted roof. The capitals of the pillars here are also finely carved with foliage; in typically Decorated style, flatter than the deeply-cut foliage of the preceding Early English style.

Unusual in a village church, the transepts here have aisles – this format was usually reserved for cathedrals. (Considering the church's grandeur, it is somewhat surprising that the church lacks clerestory windows – although these are more a feature of the 15th, rather than the 14th century.) There were once three chapels in the south transept; their three piscinas remain in the east wall, but only the altar of the central one remains. Above it has been placed a much weathered statue of the Virgin and Child, recently brought here from the east wall outside. Hanging from the vaulted roof above is something very unusual – a hollow, square stone boss, carved with figures. It once might have held a relic or perhaps a watch light.

The crossing is separated from the chancel by a screen reconstructed largely from old wood (the rood loft has gone). The chancel itself has a colourful modern reredos behind the altar, but of historic note are the sedilia and piscina on the south wall. Facing them, on the north wall, is an ornate, ogee-arched Easter Sepulchre, in which the sacrament was placed during Holy Week. Not many of these remain to be seen. The bottom level is carved with sleeping Roman soldiers; above them, Christ – flanked by angels – steps out of his tomb.

**On the A1033, 16 miles (25.5 km)
south-east of Hull
(map page 58)**

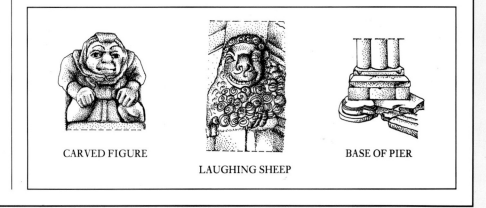

CARVED FIGURE

LAUGHING SHEEP

BASE OF PIER

Continued from page 123

Inside, the robust chevron decoration on the arches at the crossing, a motif beloved of Norman masons, stands out in the gloom. The font is in fact the base of a cross, dated around AD 1000, modified not in ancient days, but in the 19th century. There is a grand Celtic cross of similar date to the font in the south transept.

At the eastern corner of Anglesey,
4 miles (6.5 km) north-east of Beaumaris
(map page 58)

◆

PICKERING NORTH YORKSHIRE
ST PETER AND ST PAUL

It is difficult to pierce the veil of the Reformation and imagine the vivid church of medieval days. The 15th-century murals here help.

This church has both Norman and Decorated elements: there are fine Decorated sedilia in the chancel, and Decorated windows. And though the Victorians restored it, the pre-Reformation wall paintings escaped – for they did not scrape the old plaster from the walls. The paintings were hidden at the time, whitewashed at the Reformation (and afterwards by the Georgians who fastened funeral hatchments through them). After four centuries of oblivion, they were discovered during repairs in 1851, when the vicar wanted to destroy them on the grounds that they were worthless as works of art, popish in their general intention and likely to distract the congregation. Luckily, his archbishop ruled against this, and a fresh coat of whitewash simply removed them from sight. They were uncovered and restored about 100 years ago.

They cover the north and south walls of the nave, above the Norman arches (it is worth bringing binoculars) and were probably painted when these walls were heightened and the clerestory inserted in 1450. They include scenes from the lives of Jesus and the saints, then believed by Catholics to be able to intercede to save sinners from damna-

Left *The Norman south doorway at Penmon*

tion. On the north wall St Christopher, the patron saint of travellers, appears in his usual place opposite the main (here south) door – those setting off could commend themselves to him before leaving. Beside St Christopher, St George kills the Dragon. The martyrdoms of St John the Baptist and St Thomas à Becket are depicted (note that his murderers are in 15th-century rather than Norman armour). Below Thomas à Becket, St Edmund appears tied to a tree and pierced with arrows.

The south wall shows the story of St Catherine of Alexandria, martyred on a wheel (hence the Catherine wheel firework); and the Seven Acts of Mercy – which include feeding the hungry, clothing the naked and visiting those in prison. Between two arches is a striking 'Harrowing of Hell' – foremost amongst the souls (all wearing modesty discs) is Adam who hands the apple to Christ.

15 miles (24 km) west of Scarborough,
on the A170 (map page 58)

◆

RIVENHALL ESSEX
ST MARY AND ALL SAINTS

Many country churches hold unexpected treasures, and this seemingly modest church is certainly one of them. It appears to be Victorian, but its smooth face (stucco without, plaster within) conceals sturdy Saxon walls made of flint rubble and Roman tiles. It has a two-cell plan of nave and chancel: only extensions to the chancel and the tower at the west end depart from this simple layout.

Outside, on the north wall of the chancel, the facing has been removed to reveal Saxon work. The narrow, round-headed window high up in the wall is single-splayed in Norman style, though radio-carbon dating of its wooden sill suggests that it is pre-Conquest. (It is often difficult to be dogmatic about dating 'style'.) Within the church, other early features can be seen – part of a medieval wall painting near the pulpit; some 12th-century stone coffin lids in the chancel. There are also funeral hatchments and box pews from much later, Georgian times. It is a good church to

browse in, but it is worth more than a casual visit – for it contains some of the oldest stained glass in Europe. The unique panels were bought by the assistant curate in 1840, and are fitted into the east window.

The tall, willowy figures in the glass from a church in the Touraine resemble those in windows in Chartres Cathedral, which are firmly dated to 1150 – the similarities include the way the cushions are cross-hatched (they resemble tennis rackets).

This east window also holds some good late medieval French glass; there is more in the south nave window, and 16th- and some 17th-century Flemish glass in the north nave window.

All this glass survived an earthquake in 1884, and was buried for safety in World War II.

8 miles (13 km) north-east of the edge
of Chelmsford, off the A12 at Rivenhall
End (map page 57)

◆

ST BRIAVELS GLOUCESTERSHIRE
St Mary

The setting alone, 900 ft (270 m) above the Wye valley, makes a visit to this church worthwhile.

This cruciform church, dating from 1086, keeps many interesting features, despite considerable Victorian restoration (the tower dates from around 1830). The nave arcades provide a comparison between Norman (south) and Early English with tall pointed 'fishhead' arches (north), while those of the chancel and transepts are somewhat earlier 'Transitional'. The Norman capitals are each differently carved, while the Early English are fluted octagons. The font, with its unusual stone frill, is also Norman.

The Victorians broke up fine Early English windows in the north transept and Lady Chapel, and set a piscina from the north transept into the north wall of the chancel, ignoring its original function for the ritual washing of vessels and

Left The cruciform church at St Briavels

hands alongside the altar. However, the 'restorers' did rescue a stone slab dated 1272 from under the floor; it is now in the Lady Chapel.

St Briavel was a 5th-century Celtic saint who lived before St Augustine's arrival, and led a religious community in the valley behind the church. Churches' dedications to saints are usually pre-Reformation, reflecting the Catholic belief in saintly intercession. St Peter was popular as he held the keys to heaven, but many churches opted for safety with All Saints. St Briavel was a prior dedication here.

7 miles (11 km) north of Chepstow, on
the B4228 (map pages 56–7)

◆

ST MARGARET'S HEREFORD AND WORCESTER
St Margaret

This small, isolated church with its weather-boarded bell turret stands high up, with magnificent views across turbulent border country – there are Norman castles to the north, west and south. The original church was also Norman, and keeps its simple two-cell plan of nave and chancel. It is plastered throughout, adding to its simple appeal. Written wall texts remain in the chancel and behind the pulpit.

The real wonder of the church, which is worth a long journey to see, is the wooden rood assembly dated about 1520. It would have been richly coloured, but its intricate carving is magnificent enough without. The wide rood loft was used as a gallery for musicians and singers; the front is divided into panels, and it is embellished top and bottom with foliage friezes and other decoration. Its underside has moulded ribs with bosses carved with heads (one man has his tongue out), lions and shields. This loft is supported by two posts, also richly decorated with lacelike carvings (there is no 'screen' as such).

Luckily, whether to include the screen in the Reformation order to destroy all religious images was left to the discretion of the parish, and though the rood itself has gone, as have the figures of Mary and St John the Baptist that were in the niches in the pillars, the rood assembly itself remains.

A sign of the days when the church was the centre of community life can be seen in an unusual detail. The game of fives or handball used to be played against the outside of the north wall of the nave; hinges for shutters protecting the east window remain.

About 10 miles (16 km) west of
Hereford, 1 mile (1.5 km) west of the
B4347 (map page 56)

◆

SALL NORFOLK
St Peter and St Paul

Many fine Perpendicular wool churches are to be found in what are today small sleepy villages. Sall's tower now dominates mainly fields, but the village was once a thriving wool and weaving settlement, with six trade guilds, each with (until the Reformation) its own chantry altar in the church.

The church is almost entirely early and mid 15th-century, but the top stage of the tower with its ornate battlements and pinnacles was added at the end of that century. Many features of such churches were donated by wealthy merchant families, and the chancel stalls were for these

The splendid Perpendicular wool church at Sall

patrons, not for a choir. The south transept, for example, was added by a Thomas Brigg who died in 1444. It was a chantry; Thomas willed to have three chaplains celebrate here for 25 years after his death, and the transept's east window commemorates him and his two wives, Margaret and Margaret.

The tall arcades between nave and aisles are exquisitely graceful. Above the high clerestory is not the usual hammer-beam roof, but a daring alternative, where the weight of the roof is bled down through both nave and aisle walls – the arched braces stand on the ends of the main rafters of the aisle roofs, which have been brought through the walls of the nave.

The church was finished in about 1500. By 1552 the Reformation commissioners were making an inventory of what was 'superstitious' and had to be destroyed. Only faint echoes remain of the glory of the rood screen, its lower part (with saw marks visible) still carrying paintings of apostles. The tall, ornate font and cover has been defaced, but is still spectacular.

About 12 miles (19 km) north-east of
East Dereham, just north of the B1145
(map page 57)

◆

SELBORNE HAMPSHIRE
St Mary

This spacious church has been well restored and provides pleasing examples of early stages of building development. The great piers of the nave, for example, are Norman in style, but the arches which spring from them are 'Transitional' – they are pointed, plain and without moulding, and mark the step between Norman and Early English (see pages 19–22). Early English style was characterized by simple lancet window openings, and these can be seen in the south aisle.

The excellent restoration provided the noble chancel arch echoing the Transitional arches of the nave, and the lancets above the altar. The east window of the south aisle has its lancets grouped together, a move towards the Decorated window (see page 24).

But this church is really notable for another reason. Gilbert White, one of the fathers of natural history, was once curate here (in fact it was his great-nephew William White who designed both the chancel arch and the chancel's lancet windows).

Gilbert White's letters to friends – inquisitive and filled with affection for the countryside around him – were published in 1789 as *The Natural History and Antiquities of Selborne*. The book is so popular that it has never been out of print.

He knew the old yew in the churchyard of course; it was toppled in the Great Storm of January 1990, but efforts have been made to right it. Strangely, although he describes a giant old oak that had stood in the village before he was born, he seems to have taken the churchyard yew for granted and makes no mention of it. Gilbert White's unpretentious gravestone is just to the north of the chancel, marked with the simple inscription 'G.W. 26th June 1793'. Perhaps a more fitting memorial is the 1920s St Francis window at the east end of the south aisle, which shows the saint preaching to the birds mentioned in Gilbert White's book. In the background are the church, the great yew and the vicarage where Gilbert White was born.

Note the single-handed church clock.

4 miles (6.5 km) south-east of Alton, on
the B3006 (map page 57)

SHOBDON   HEREFORD AND WORCESTER
St John the Evangelist

The decorative curves of the ogee arches on the doors and windows of this plain exterior are clues to a really remarkable 'rococo' interior of what is in plan a simple, sober, mid 18th-century Georgian church.

The style is often called 'Strawberry Hill Gothic' after the famous house built by Horace Walpole on the Thames at Twickenham. The colour is muted, the interior all painted in white and restrained blue. Even the pews are white, lined with blue, and the ironwork screens dividing the nave from the chancel and the transepts are also painted white.

The decoration is 'Gothic' with rococo additions. This can be seen at the pew ends, for example, where an arching top is pierced by a Gothic quatrefoil surrounded by rococo scrolls. The shape of these scrolls is echoed by the curves of the off-hanging arches of chancel and transepts, which are wholly ornamental; they have no structural function whatever, and they are decorated with crockets.

All that is left of the older church here is the tower which was added to the Norman building in the 13th century, and the Norman font, with lions carved on its stem, which is back where it belongs after being used as a garden ornament.

The Norman church had exquisitely decorated doorways and other decoration of the kind seen at Kilpeck (Hereford and Worcester). When the old building was being demolished, the two doorways and the chancel arch were 'rescued' and placed as a folly about a quarter of a mile north of the church, where they can still be seen, badly weathered. Was it folly to pull down a masterpiece of Norman work, and build the masterpiece we see today?

6 miles (9.5 km) west of Leominster, on
the B4362 (map pages 56–7)

SOMPTING   WEST SUSSEX
St Mary

This church's outstanding Saxon tower has typical windows, but is unique because it retains its original four-gabled roofing, the only remaining English example of a 'Rhenish Helm' (or Rhineland helmet). Wooden shingles hide the Saxon timbering.

The tower walls are flint rubble with patches of plastering remaining. Thin (matchstick) stone strips run down each side, and the cornerings seem much less massive than at Breamore (Hampshire) because the horizontal stones of the 'long-and-short' work have been cut back to the width of the uprights. These strips of stone – and the horizontal one

St Mary's, Sompting, with its unique 'Rhenish Helm'

at the level of the nave eaves – echo timber construction, with which the Saxons were familiar. Inside the tower is a Saxon arch with carved leaf capitals.

In Norman times the church was granted to the Knights Templars; instead of converting it into a round church (see LITTLE MAPLESTEAD, Essex), they rebuilt the nave and chancel on the Saxon foundations and added the north and south transepts for their private use.

Both of these transepts are interesting. The north has what were probably two small chapels on its east side, the southern of which would have served as the 'chancel' for this area. The south transept also has its own miniature chancel and sacristy. The Templars, wealthy and exempt from all taxes, would find a strong-room essential. Thus each transept formed a separate knightly church of an unusual kind.

There are one or two pieces of Saxon carving inserted into the Norman fabric, such as the strips over the piscina in the chancel. The carving of an abbot, or bishop, in the south transept, and the tendril arching above, imitates manuscript illustration. The rather odd anatomy is typical.

A ruined, freestanding medieval chapel lies to the north-west of the main church. A new parish room has been built inside. In time the Templars fell from grace, partly because of accusations of corruption, and their properties were assigned to the Hospitallers, who turned over the whole of this church to the local people, but built this extra chapel for their own use.

On the western outskirts of Lancing,
just south of the A27 (map page 57)

STANFORD ON AVON NORTHAMPTONSHIRE
ST NICHOLAS

Rather solitary, barely claiming a village, this church is well worth a detour. It is spacious inside, with 17 Georgian funeral hatchments making bold decoration. Although it was largely rebuilt in the 14th century, some unusual early Norman work was found in 1909. Above a chancel roof of reed and plaster, the main roof beams are the well-matched boughs of a great oak tree, hardly trimmed by adze. The stalls by the low window in the south wall of the chancel are also adze trimmed. The panelling here is Elizabethan and the plain oak altar table is of interest – it was used by William Laud who came here as vicar in 1607, and rose to be Archbishop of Canterbury and a powerful figure opposed to the later development of the Reformation (he was hostile to Puritanism). To the north of the altar is one of the church's many handsome tombs bearing the effigies of a couple and eight of their children, dated 1613.

The east window is especially interesting – its glass glows with intense feeling. The top half dates to early in the 14th century. The five lower panels, of a somewhat later date, were discovered in a chest in Stanford Hall in 1932. They fitted the lower lights of the window exactly, and had been removed to save them from Puritan destruction.

The charming Renaissance organ is also worth a journey: traditionally, it once belonged to King Charles I, and stood in the Chapel Royal at Whitehall Palace. But after the King's execution, it was sold off by Oliver Cromwell, and eventually made its way here. At its top is a mitre surmounted by a crown, symbolic of the belief in the Divine Right of Kings to rule – a belief which brought both Charles I and Archbishop Laud to the scaffold.

Considerable conservation and restoration work is taking place in this magnificent church.

About 6 miles (9.5 km) north-east of
Rugby, 1½ miles (2.5 km) south of the
B5414 (map page 57)

STAUNTON HAROLD   LEICESTERSHIRE
HOLY TRINITY

This parkland church, in its walled churchyard and over-looking the lake, was the chapel of the great hall nearby; it is now in the care of the National Trust.

One of the few churches built during the Commonwealth, it was founded in 1653 by Sir Robert Shirley in open defiance of the Puritans. For him it was, as the inscription over the west door states, a time 'when all thinges Sacred were throughout ye nation Either demolisht or profaned'. For this belief he was sent to the Tower of London.

Staunton Harold rejected both Papism and Puritanism, and expressed the 'High Church' Anglicanism of Charles I and his Royalist followers. The 16th-century Protestant Reformers and the 17th-century Puritans both held that holy images and the Mass itself were forbidden by God and idolatrous. But another – less radical – school of thought had grown up, which wanted the old Catholic religion reformed, rather than destroyed. This 'High Church' revived Gothic style, and restored the altar, furnished again with the candlesticks and plate that the Puritans had destroyed, to the east end, behind rails. These are sometimes known as Laudian rails after William Laud, who became Archbishop of Canterbury in 1663. This 'step back' further incensed the Puritans, and helped fan the discontent which led to the Civil War and Commonwealth.

The body of this church is a 'Gothic survival' with a medley of features – a 'Decorated' east window, for example, but low-pitched roofs, battlements and tower of Perpendicular character.

Inside, the carved woodwork is of firmly 17th-century, Jacobean character. The pulpit, lectern, box pews, panelling and screens are all the work of one craftsman. The altar is back at the end of the chancel, which is empty of seating and used only by communicants: the service was conducted from a desk in the nave.

Also of interest is the rather fine 17th-century 'organ loft' gallery, and the wooden ceiling, painted in 1655 to represent the Creation.

3 miles (5 km) north-east of Ashby de la
Zouch, west of the B587 (map page 57)

STOW   LINCOLNSHIRE
ST MARY

In about AD 975 an Anglo-Saxon minster was built here, a mother church to serve a block of church estates. Although largely destroyed by fire, it was rebuilt before the Norman Conquest. Today's nave and chancel are Norman work, but the Saxon crossing between them survives. The church is interesting architecturally because the side porticus are the same height as the nave and chancel – a step beyond the low ones at BREAMORE (Hampshire) towards true transepts. The plain Perpendicular tower above the crossing replaced a wooden Saxon original.

The outside is rather staid; the trio of windows on the

The church of St Mary at Stow

133

The churches of St Cyriac (foreground) and St Mary stand together in one churchyard at Swaffham Prior

south wall of the south transept is of interest – one a Saxon slit, one a round Norman window, and one 13th-century early Gothic of two lancets with a quatrefoil above.

The south doorway is Norman, alive with chevron and other decoration, but even this gives little idea of the massive architectural splendour to be found inside. The nave keeps the height typical of Celtic-influenced Saxon churches. The vast Saxon arch at the east end of the nave is greater in scale than any other in Britain.

Beyond it lies the crossing, and it is now clear that the rather plain tower supported on pointed inner arches has been built within the base of the original round-arched Saxon tower. The Saxon doorway to the north transept has long-and-short side stonework and an irregular arrangement of the stones creating the curve of the arch above.

The spacious Norman chancel was quite well restored by the Victorians, except for the floor tiles. The floor memorial on the south side carries an inscription, perhaps of 1300, which reads (in part in mirror writing): 'Alle men that ben in lif, prai for Emme was Fuk wif' (Fulk's wife). On the south pier of the chancel arch is a 10th-century graffito of a Viking ship. Other features of this splendid place are the 15th-century pews on the north side of the nave, the font, and the ring of six bells, which has not been retuned and so keeps its primitive sound.

9 miles (14.5 km) north-west of
Lincoln, on the B1241 (map pages 57–8)

◆

SWAFFHAM PRIOR CAMBRIDGESHIRE
St Mary and St Cyriac

In this attractive village with many thatched cottages, two churches stand in the one churchyard. There are folk-tales that the competitive pride of two neighbouring lords of the manor forced them each to build a church. In fact, the two recall a time when today's village was divided into two parishes, and the site presumably offered an island of solid ground, secure from floods, in the then largely undrained fenny countryside.

St Mary's, the church with the staged tower, is still in use as the parish church. The massive flint and rubble tower is an interesting construction: the bottom stage is square with an octagonal second stage on it. These lower stages are Norman, while the two top 16-sided stages are of Early English date. They were struck by lightning in 1767.

The tower of St Cyriac's is in good repair. Its church, although the original 12th-century building was restored in the last century, is no longer used and is in decay. The tower has an arrangement unusual for the Perpendicular, of an octagonal upper stage rising from the square base, and topped with a decorative parapet.

8 miles (13 km) north-east of
Cambridge, on the B1102
(map page 57)

◆

TICKHILL SOUTH YORKSHIRE
St Mary

A tall western tower is often a clue that a church underwent major rebuilding in the 15th century. Here, the fine Perpendicular upper stages added at that time rise on a massively buttressed tower dating from the 13th century. The niches retain their original, but decayed, statues, and the tower terminates in an exuberantly decorated crown with an unusual lacelike fretted parapet.

Much of the money for such improvements came from bequests by the wealthy wool and textile traders; here in 1429, John Sandford left 100 shillings, a cart and four horses, 'to the makyng of the stepell of Tyckhill' (the word 'stepell' is used here in its meaning of a tall tower; Perpendicular towers did not generally have spires).

Over a period, the great west window was installed and the east window in the chancel enlarged, the aisles were widened and given larger windows, and a clerestory was put in, as was an additional window over the chancel arch. The nave arcades were remodelled, and porches added to the outside.

There were four chantries, separated enclosures with

their own altars, in which masses were said to release the donor's soul from purgatory. A typical chantry stood in the chapel north of the chancel, founded in 1348. The income to pay the priest came from an endowment of 27 acres, one large house and eight cottages. Five priests or more would have been needed to service the altars of this particular church.

Much of this was swept away at the Reformation. Some fragments of coloured glass dating from about 1485 do remain in windows in the south aisle – with apostles holding scrolls with parts of the creed in Latin. The rag-bag of fragments includes parts of faces reinserted every which way, even upside down!

There is also some unfortunate Victorian glass – such as the 'Faith, Hope and Charity' of 1881 in the north aisle. A more positive Victorian contribution is the carved alabaster monument to a mother and child near the north-west corner of the church, which is most moving.

9 miles (14.5 km) east of Rotherham,
on the A361 (map page 58)

UP HOLLAND   LANCASHIRE
ST THOMAS

A few great parish churches were not built as such, but formed part of a monastic centre; at the Dissolution of the Monasteries, they were adopted for parish use. EDINGTON (Wiltshire) survives as a whole, but here in Up Holland the impressive nave was in fact the chancel/choir of a priory founded in 1317. The tall, slender, late Decorated pillars date from this period, whereas the western tower was added (where the crossing tower would have been in the original) in the 15th or 16th century. It has a splendid doorway, although the figures and heads which decorated it have been defaced. The present chancel was added in the 1880s.

The benches are dated to 1635, and are interesting, since box pews (rather than benches) were becoming increasingly popular at that time. There is an uncommon, special pew for the churchwardens, dated 1679.

It is quite a well-lit church, showing to advantage the attractive plasterwork ceiling dating from 1752.

5 miles (8 km) west of Wigan, on the
A577 (map page 58)

WARHAM ST MARY   NORFOLK
ST MARY

This is one of the few churches that escaped the zealous attentions of the Victorian restorers and ecclesiologists. Its exterior, with a Decorated tower, Perpendicular battlements and some Perpendicular windows, gives no hint of the delight of the interior.

Framed by clean walls, and below a shallowly curving ceiling, its furnishings are what are known as 'Prayer Book' – with 18th-century box pews, and a three-decker pulpit with a tester or sounding board above to beam the sermon down to the congregation. The pulpit dominates the nave of this relatively small church. The font resembles nothing so much as a bird bath. The Royal Arms of George III are here painted on to canvas. There are hat pegs, presumably of the same 18th-century date as the furniture, on the north wall of the nave.

It was much loved in the 19th century – the Reverend Langton in 1801 'beautified' the interior with glass he had collected, which includes Flemish Renaissance and English medieval pieces.

2 miles (3 km) south-east of Wells-next-
the-Sea, off the B1105 (map page 57)

WARKWORTH   NORTHUMBERLAND
ST LAWRENCE

Both Danes and Scots regularly raided this coast; and this still fairly complete Norman church was a place of sanctuary as well as worship. It was built like a fortress, if never as strong as the castle which faces it at the opposite

Warham St Mary – one of the few churches to escape over-zealous Victorian restorers

The Norman church at Warkworth

end of the broad street. Unfortunately for the inhabitants, it was not strong enough to resist the forces of Duncan, Earl of Fife, in 1174, who massacred 300 local people who had taken refuge there.

The church has a long narrow nave and chancel enclosed by thick stone walls. Externally, its original Norman face is best seen from the north, the nave wall here having broad flat buttresses and plain windows. The western tower and spire, and south aisle, were medieval additions. The piers of the south nave arcade follow the line of the Norman south wall, but the Norman chancel arch is still standing, although awry. The chancel has been sensitively restored to its original form, with the Norman stone-vaulted roof reinforced by ribs decorated with chevron – Warkworth is one of the few country churches to have a vaulted chancel. There are fragments of Celtic crosses in the chancel and the effigy of a 14th-century knight, holding his heart between his hands. The face is quite finely carved.

Also worth a visit (via a ferry: apply to the castle for admission) is nearby Warkworth hermitage, a small 14th-century chapel cut out of the cliff above the River Coquet, with an imitation vaulted roof and an altar carved from the rock. A figure carved in a recess represents a woman. Legend

has it that she is Lady Isabel of Widdrington, who was accidentally killed by her lover, Sir Bertram, who spent his life in penance, carving out the chapel from the rock. (His lodgings, at the cliff top, are more comfortable.)

7 miles (11 km) south-east of Alnwick,
on the A1068 (map page 58)

---◆---

WEST WALTON NORFOLK
St Mary

This is one of the best Early English churches in Britain, begun in 1225. Its tower stands, unusually, about 60 ft (18 m) from the church, presumably seeking out firmer ground. Its open arches at the base allow it to be used as a lych gate – an Italian fashion but unusual in Britain.

Early English was the first pure Gothic style. The south porch (ignore the brick gable above the doorway which is a 16th-century addition) achieves its effect with a minimum of fanciful decoration – the dogtooth is enough.

The interior is magnificent, with delicately poised nave arcades. Everything is drawn with firm lines – in the tall narrow-pointed arches, in the columns with their separate shafts, 'tied together' with shaft-rings. This is typical Early English work, as are the deeply-cut leafy capitals. In this church the rhythm of the arcades is extended by the clerestory windows above. The 'tapestry' effect was painted on the clerestory walls in the 13th century, and the roundels were repainted in the 18th century with emblems of the tribes of Israel. Only the seating is clumsy in this setting; in later times taller bases to the pillars might take seating into account.

The hammer-beam roof is a fine one, but does not fit very well; it might have come from another church and been adapted. The chancel, too, has been adapted – it was shortened in 1807 and its east window is modern; but an unusual feature remains with the eight sedilia (four in the north wall and four in the south), a reminder of a Cluniac priory cell which was founded in the village soon after the

Norman Conquest. It numbered 11 men, and at High Mass eight would sit, with the other three officiating at the altar.

Such cells were not only religious, but also highly commercial; records show that this one held the rights to a fair and market, and was responsible for wrecks, gallows and the quality of bread and beer consumed locally.

The great 15th-century font raised on three octagonal stone steps at the west end of the nave is also a dramatic feature.

About 2 miles (3 km) north-east of
Wisbech, west of the A47 (map page 57)

WESTWELL KENT
St Mary

This is a splendidly atmospheric village church, largely Early English in style but with a delightful quirk or two. The tower, nave and chancel are mid 13th-century, and the tower arch with its carved capitals is a special feature. Within the tower, the old oak ladder leads to the belfry, with four 17th-century bells. Sadly, due to the weakness of the belfry timbers, they have not rung for years.

The north and south aisles, each with its own gabled roof, are 14th-century. Their windows give a clear illustration of the evolution of Gothic styles: those of the north are of three dates – two are original single Early English lancets, one is two-lighted Decorated and four are three-lighted Perpendicular.

The pointed arches of the aisle arcades rest on pillars which are alternately round and octagonal; and typical of the time. Any reason for this alternation, other than for decorative purposes, has been forgotten. Unusually, this line of arches marches on through the chancel. The triple chancel arch is unusual, with round slender pillars which lead up to cusped heads – that is, to trefoil-headed arches.

In the chancel is another glory of this church: fine sedilia for officiating priests, above which is the head of a king, perhaps Henry III, with his queen on the facing wall.

Above the altar is a 13th-century window, of three lancets, the centre showing the Jesse Tree, the descent of Jesus from David. The glass in the upper part here is from the 13th century, the lower recently restored in the same style from scraps of old glass. In 1987 the whole was dismantled and cleaned. The altar was installed in September 1989, modern in style but designed to complement the stone reredos behind.

The 12th-century font and old oak south door are also of interest.

3 miles (5 km) north of Ashford, east of
the A20 (map page 57)

WEST WYCOMBE BUCKINGHAMSHIRE
St Laurence

The church stands on top of a yew-covered hill, within an Iron Age hillfort (the ditches are much reduced). Alongside is a huge and unusual hexagonal mausoleum, built in 1756, dotted with urns and columns and loosely derived from Constantine's Arch in Rome. At about the same time, parts of the church were rebuilt from the 13th-century original. This was commissioned by Sir Francis Dashwood, owner of the estate, who was notorious as an eccentric, and a leading light of the Hell-Fire Club, whose orgies were sometimes held in the caves cut into the hill beneath.

The striking golden ball at the top of the tower can seat four people to enjoy the spectacular view, but the interior of the church is even more exotic, for the nave was fashioned on the 5th-century BC Temple of the Sun at Palmyra. It is a great ballroom of a space, 60 ft (18 m) long and 40 ft (12 m) wide, along whose walls march 16 massive, red-painted, Corinthian columns carrying a painted ceiling, while the walls carry ponderous stucco swags of foliage and flowers. It was reckoned to be among the most beautiful churches of its age.

The open benches of the nave suit the style of the church. There is an odd assemblage of thrones – two reading desks and another, very comfortably padded with a small eagle

reading desk on a stem in front of it, which probably served as the pulpit.

The movable font (which may be in the chancel when you visit) is equally bizarre – from a base of three claws rises a tall narrow stem up which a serpent writhes in chase of a dove. Four other doves stand around the bowl above, as if at a birdbath!

Although the chancel, which is now somewhat blocked off by the altar, is from the 13th-century building, it was remodelled inside in the 1760s, with, among other things, decorative stucco and ceiling paintings. The communion table, stalls and reredos are of the same time.

About 1 mile (1.5 km) west of High
Wycombe, to the north of the A40
(map page 57)

WHITBY NORTH YORKSHIRE
ST MARY

The church is set among gravestones and table tombs with the ruined abbey alongside, on a hill overlooking the harbour. The Synod of Whitby was convened somewhere near here in AD 664 (see page 11), but the oldest parts of this sturdy building (squat tower, south doorway and chancel) are 12th-century Norman.

This gives no clue to the inside, which was all, except for the chancel, refurnished in the 17th and 18th centuries and forgotten by Victorian restorers. As you enter below a western gallery, sheer confusion seems to reign: box pews lead one to another, seeming to cover the floor; and galleries range around the walls at many different levels. There is even a 'flying pew', raised on twisting barley-sugar columns, crossing the Norman chancel arch in place of the rood screen and loft.

This all echoes the Protestant belief that the congregation should face and be in clear view of the reading desk, from which the lessons were read, and the pulpit. Here pulpit

Left *Caedron's Cross stands before St Mary's, Whitby*

and reading desk are combined – and in spite of the apparent jumble, all the congregation can see the pulpit easily.

On the coast, 20 miles (32 km) north-
west of Scarborough (map page 58)

WICKHAM BERKSHIRE
ST SWITHUN

The tower is Saxon; it stands at the south-west of the church, its walls of flint with copious mortar, and with long-and-short work at the corners. It was, like many of that time, also designed as a watch-tower – the blocked doorway part-way up the side is the watchman's entrance, which could be reached by ladder. At the top of the tower, holes are set in the walls, possibly to take beams on which a warning beacon could be lit.

Much of the rest of the building was restored in the 1840s – in parts extravagantly, such as the very expensive square knapped (broken) flint work which greets you on the way to the south porch. The organ was another expensive addition – it cost £1000 in 1842. This sum was then a small fortune, and is an indication of the expenditure that the Victorians considered suitable for their churches. Also extravagant, but mischievous, are the elephants' heads 'supporting' the roof of the north aisle. The nave has more conventional angel corbels, but the restorer acquired four papier mâché elephants' heads from the Paris Exhibition of 1862, had four more made, and mounted the set here.

Also of interest is the *chasuble* (a circular cape worn by officiating priests at Mass) in a glass case, which is possibly one mentioned in parish records for 1552. Saxon and Norman churches were Romanesque, a style that was strongly linked with Byzantium. That link remained strong in the vestments worn at services, and continues today.

6 miles (9.5 km) north-west of Newbury,
on the B4000 (map page 57)

Guided Tour

WHITCHURCH CANONICORUM DORSET
ST CANDIDA (ST WITE) AND HOLY CROSS

Set in a tree-lined churchyard in the corner of the Marshwood Vale, disturbed only by the cawing of the rooks, this handsome church contains exquisite Early English features. The village takes its name from the church; the word Canonicorum, meaning 'of the Canons', refers to the fact that the church's tithes were taken over by the Cathedral Chapters of Sarum and Wells in the 13th century. This is the only parish church in England to retain the relics and shrine of its saint – it was once an important place for pilgrimage.

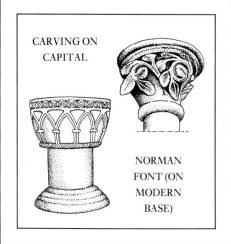

CARVING ON CAPITAL

NORMAN FONT (ON MODERN BASE)

The tall tower is 14th-century Perpendicular. It and the older nave walls are both of mellowed lichen-patched stone – apart from the modern winsome figure in the southern-facing niche of the tower. High on the south side of the tower walls are two interesting carved panels, one depicting an axe and Viking longboat and the other showing an axe and an adze. Both may relate to the legend of St Wite, as we shall see. On the exterior nave wall, to the west of the porch, between the two windows, is a carving of a two-handled chalice (supposedly the Holy Grail) of the kind used in Norman times. The Sanctus bell turret at the east end of the nave is one of the few left by the Puritans.

The porch is 14th-century, but protects a Norman-cum-Transitional doorway, its modest decoration including a single row of dogtooth and a single central beakhead. There are pilgrim crosses cut into the right-hand (east) jamb of the door. The font is Norman (apart from its modern base) and probably the original; it carries shallow, but beautiful decoration of interlacing arches between borders of stars (resembling dogtooth) and cable. It was found in a field nearby in 1845.

The tall arch to the tower was cut when the latter was built in around 1400: the panelled decoration of its underface is found only in the West Country (the tran-

sept arches are similar). The barrel vault of the nave (and that of the north transept) dates from this time. Compare the south and north arches of the nave; the sunken and leaning Norman pillars of the south reflect serious subsidence problems, and the north arcade obviously had to be replaced. Its finely pointed arches are Early English and their decoration is a remarkable testimony to the imagination of that time. One arch has chevron ornament, others are plain. But the delicate, clustered shafts have beautiful, deep-cut capitals; all variations of foliage.

Similar foliage is repeated on the capitals of chancel and transept arches. The lovely arch between south aisle and south transept is also of this time. (Much of the south transept is obscured by the organ; but note the hatchment with its quaint poem above the vestry door.) The chancel arch is Early English, but the east, lancet windows here date (as do the quatrefoil clerestory windows of the nave) from the 19th century. The linenfold panelling of the carved choir stalls is also Victorian. The memorials here are of interest, especially the grandiose tomb near the altar, dating from 1611, of Sir John Jefferey. The oak pulpit dates from Stuart times.

The north transept, lit by deeply splayed Early English lancet windows on the side walls, once contained two altars. Today there is one, its altar slab reclaimed from the floor where it had been embedded, upside down, at the Reformation. This transept also contains the church's greatest treasure: the 13th-century shrine of St Wite. How it survived the Reformation is a mystery.

The saint's relics (a number of bones, thought to be a woman's) lie within the plain stone tomb chest. Diseased limbs, or bandages taken from the afflicted, were thrust into three oval openings; today there are often notes or prayers to be found in them.

———

The 14th-century church tower is a fine example of the Perpendicular style

There is little certain about St Wite. One tradition is that she was a Saxon woman killed by Danish raiders. Another is that she fled from Norse pirates by walking on water, but in escaping had two fingers hacked off by an axe – hence, perhaps, the panels on the tower. The church is known as St Candida rather than St Wite, Candida being the Latin word for white (perhaps a mistranslation of the Saxon Wite). There are also Breton tradi-

tions of a saintly Blanche (French for white) and a Celtic Gwen, who has been identified with her. Many Bretons fled to the west of England, bringing their Christian traditions and relics with them – perhaps including the bones of Blanche/Gwen.

4 miles (6.5 km) north-east of Lyme Regis, about 1 mile (1.5 km) north of the A35 (map page 56)

The Saxon stone church at Wing

WING BUCKINGHAMSHIRE
ALL SAINTS

At first sight this church does not seem unusual, but well proportioned and with windows and battlements of typical Perpendicular style. It is at heart, however, one of the finest remaining Saxon stone churches in Britain.

It was of basilican plan, an aisled nave with an apse. The 10th-century Saxon work includes the nave, north aisle, the chancel arch and the apse. Typically Saxon is the fact that the nave 'arcades' are not arches springing from rounded piers or columns as they would be at later dates, but of doorways pierced through the wall. The great chancel arch is one of the widest Saxon arches in Britain. Above it is a paired Saxon window. Facing this, at the other end of the nave, are Saxon doorways (discovered in 1954) high in the walls. These once led to a private chapel or gallery, perhaps for the use of local thegns or important visitors.

The outside of the apse is worth inspecting – it is of rather regular stonework; above the decoration of blind arches is the shadow of the original triangular window heads.

Wing was clearly an important place; and below the chancel is a crypt, reached by stairs from the outside. If the door is locked, something of the impressive vaulting can still be seen through the grille. This might well be two centuries older than the rest of the building, and was certainly home to sacred relics of some kind. A royal lady called Aelfgifu who died in AD 975 bequeathed her estates, including Wing Manor, to her brother-in-law, King Edgar, and mentioned 'its shrine with relics'.

Among the many funerary memorials of later centuries is the Dormer monument of 1552 in the north aisle. With fluted Corinthian columns and an ornate classical 'Italian' canopy, it is an early breath of the Renaissance in a British parish church.

10 miles (16 km) north-east of
Aylesbury, on the A418 (map page 57)

WINTERBOURNE BASSETT WILTSHIRE
ST KATHARINE AND ST PETER

This church is often described as an architectural gem; it has much in 14th-century, Decorated style. Apart from the 15th-century tower, the walls are largely built of sarsen stone, with cornerings of limestone. Sarsens are the weathered remains of a hard layer of sandstone rock which once lay on top of the older chalk. Sarsen boulders were used by prehistoric man for tombs, ritual avenues and circles, such as at Avebury, which is not far down the A4361. Although the ground was once strewn with them, they have largely been cleared away for the plough; many can be seen dumped alongside streams. However, the use of sarsens (which are difficult to work) could indicate that the stone was appropriated from a prehistoric ritual centre. Those making the north transept are very rough, and this could be the oldest part of the church.

There is one point of interest in this transept: the slab of the recessed 13th-century tomb below the fine 14th-century window shows a man and wife hand in hand. Touching though this handclasp may be, note that it is her right hand that reaches across to his. This signified that she was a considerable heiress in her own right.

There are also some fine later memorials. The chancel is also satisfying; its east window dates only from 1857, but is a good copy of a Decorated type.

The parish boundary is very old, and is virtually unchanged from that of the estate given by King Edgar to one of his ministers in AD 992.

8 miles (13 km) south-west of Swindon,
west of the A4361 (map page 57)

———————◆———————

WORTH WEST SUSSEX
ST NICHOLAS

This powerful church dates from before the Norman Conquest, perhaps from the 10th century. Victorian restorers re-roofed the nave, rebuilt the chancel and added a short tower next to the chancel to carry a short spire. But a fire in 1986 necessitated a new nave roof. This was built from scratch on pyramidal forms to reduce the stresses on the old walls. In 1989, it won the King of Prussia's Gold Medal for gifted restoration work.

The Saxon church was an ordinary 'minster' (see page 9), which in time became the parish church of what was the largest parish in Britain. In spite of the changes, the church retains its original cruciform floor plan with a curved semicircular (apsed) end to the chancel. The 'transepts', although not quite opposite each other, and although reached through doorways rather than arches, are rather more like true transepts than the small porticus of BREAMORE (Hampshire).

When the new roof was built, the solid Victorian pews were replaced by paler ones, and a nave altar placed beneath the chancel arch – probably its original position in Saxon days – with new communion rails in front. A 16th-century altar rail can be seen around the high altar at the east end of the chancel. This reached here via a London antique dealer, together with the finely carved pulpit from Germany.

Saxon two-light windows are set high in the nave. The north and south doorways retain their original Saxon arches, although the north door is blocked in. Only the bottom part of the south doorway is in use; it was originally tall enough (some say) to allow a horseman to ride in to worship without dismounting. The western doorway (though of a later date) is retained today as the main entrance. The gallery across the west end of the nave dates from 1610.

2 miles (3 km) east of the centre of
Crawley, on the B2036 (map page 57)

———————◆———————

YAXLEY CAMBRIDGESHIRE
ST PETER

There was a Saxon church here, which was enlarged in the Norman period, but the present building spans the period from 1250 to 1340. It was added to and raised over the years 1485–1540, when the tower and spire, a porch with niches for statues and posturing beasts, roofing, clerestories (to the chancel as well as the nave) and other sundry windows were installed. The spire is set well back from the parapet of the tower and supported by flying buttresses.

With wide aisles alongside the nave and chancel, and short transepts, the overall plan today is more or less rectangular. Despite the differing roof levels, the various styles live easily with each other.

St Peter's at Yaxley, enlarged in Norman times

145

Left The Saxon church at Worth, later restored

Some stylistic details are of great interest. In the end window of the north transept, stepped Early English windows have a touch of Decorated with the trefoil 'tracery', while the corresponding one in the south aisle is more firmly Decorated. The east windows of chancel and south chapel are the epitome of Decorated style.

The walls were painted at the time of the final work. Among the murals remaining are a Resurrection in the north chapel, a Doom over the chancel arch, and a grave-digger and Death (which might be late 16th-century) on the west nave wall. They are much faded. There are also traces of paintings of the nails, hammer, whip, sponge and other 'instruments of the Passion' on the screen.

In the north transept, an unusual arched panel memorial with two hands holding a heart marks a heart burial, which was found in a tubular box behind. It dates from 1293.

3 miles (5 km) south of the edge of
Peterborough, on the B1091
(map page 57)

YOULGREAVE DERBYSHIRE
ALL SAINTS

This impressive church, with its arrays of splendid battlements, is a mix of periods from Norman to Perpendicular and beyond. An interesting feature of the western tower is the outside stair-turret at its south-eastern corner. This was added in the 17th century to allow easier access to the bells (the then new skill of change ringing was becoming popular).

The wide Norman nave is impressive, with a late Norman south arcade, with typical stout piers and scalloped capitals from which spring the semicircular arches. Although only a few years later in date, the northern arcade is already showing more slender columns and more elaborate (but still Norman) capitals, carved with animal and human heads and leaf decoration. But the arches which spring from them are pointed; this is a good example of 'Transitional' work.

The church's carvings are delightful. One, from the late 12th century, is set into the wall at the west of the main nave; it may represent a pilgrim as it shows staff and purse. Another in alabaster, which was quarried nearby, is behind the north aisle altar showing a man and wife, and their 17 children, clustered around the Virgin and Child. It dates from 1492. The chancel holds the cross-legged effigy of a 14th-century knight holding his heart in his hands. Nearby is a 15th-century monument showing a knight in plate mail; because he died before his father, his effigy is only half-sized.

Most unusual is the late Norman font near the south door, consisting of a bowl (on restored shafts) with a smaller bowl at the side, carved from the same block of stone. This was perhaps used by the child's sponsors to wash their hands of the baptismal oil. The salamander carved on the underside of the font is a symbol of renewal.

3 miles (5 km) south of Bakewell, west
of the A6 (map pages 57–8)

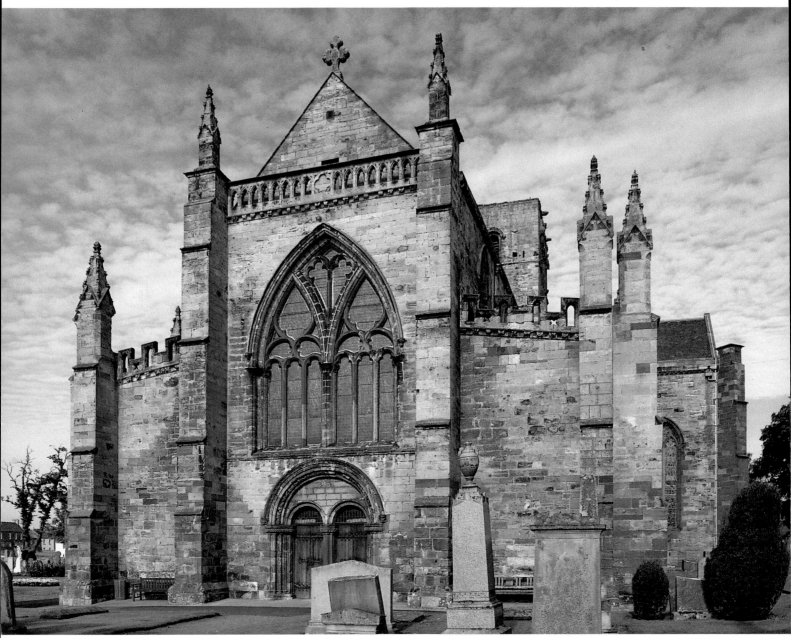

St Mary's at Haddington – the largest parish church in Scotland

3
Churches in Scotland

Three key churches – DALMENY (Lothian), DURISDEER (Dumfries and Galloway) and HADDINGTON (Lothian) – appear in the gazetteer, but here we list some others which are well worth a visit, and outline the rather different development of country churches in Scotland compared to the rest of Britain.

At first, churches in Scotland took much the same path as those further south. Celtic influence was perhaps stronger, though, and the first Celtic monastery was founded when St Columba crossed from Ireland in AD 563. It was in the west, on Iona, an island off the south-western tip of Mull (Strathclyde), but its influence spread far. The tall round tower of BRECHIN (Tayside) is Irish in influence, for example. Several churches have old Celtic crosses, such as at APPLECROSS (Highland), while many, such as RODEL (Western Isles), safeguard Celtic decorative motifs.

St Columba's simple site on Iona was later to be changed, from Norman times on, and indeed fine Norman churches are still to be found scattered across Scotland – DALMENY is one example, but there are others at LEUCHARS (Fife) and KIRKWALL (Orkney). Scotland subsequently witnessed the flowering of Decorated or High Gothic architecture, even to extreme flamboyant tracery as can be seen in the church at HADDINGTON, but not the development into Perpendicular or Late Gothic.

And with ceaseless fighting amongst the clans, it was not surprising that many churches had defensive features, such as those at CRIEFF (Tayside). CULLEN (Grampian) and ABERFELDY (Tayside) show typical 16th-century Scottish features, while BIGGAR (Strathclyde) was one of the last pre-Reformation churches built in Scotland (in 1545).

Riding on the reaction against corruption in the existing Catholic Church, the Reformation reached Scotland as well as the south. It created what was more of a community church, and in Scotland John Knox and others fashioned a Presbyterian version in which the flock chose its own minister, and which was organized nationally by a democratic General Assembly.

When the Protestant James I took the throne and became Head of the English Church, he sought to bring the Presbyterian Church into line with it, but hackles rose against the threat of outside patronage amid fears of his bishops usurping the power of the General Assembly. His successor Charles I tried to enforce the English *Book of Common Prayer*, causing riots – and many Scotsmen signed the 'National Covenant' binding them to defend the throne but to reject any outside religious pressure of this kind. Then in 1638, the Assembly took the further precautionary step of abolishing bishops in Scotland.

During the Civil War, the English Parliamentarians sought the help of the Scots Presbyters, and the latter, hoping to spread their faith south, signed the second 'Solemn League and Covenant' with the English clergy. On the execution of Charles I, his heir, later to become Charles II, was in fact adopted as King of Scotland on condition that he supported the Covenants. In the event, on his accession in 1660 he 'forgot' his promise and restored the bishops. His new Scottish Parliament removed the right of congregations to choose their own ministers and in protest many abstained, worshipping instead in secret 'conventicles' in remote areas – counted a treasonable act for which they were hunted down.

The formation of the United Kingdom in 1707, by guaranteeing Protestant succession, removed the threat of Catholic interference, but the 'clearances' of the clans from their ancestral holdings for the sake of sheep and southern profits meant that by the end of the century many old churches lay derelict. APPLECROSS is one such example. Although in time new kirks were built – some particularly interesting ones in Georgian times – church bickers continued. In 1843 dissident Scottish ministers founded their own Free Church of Scotland, giving up their manses and secure livings to do so. It was only in 1929, having again ridded itself of outside patronage, that the 'official' Church of Scotland was able to merge with this Free Church.

ABERFELDY TAYSIDE
ST MARY

This simple whitewashed church standing behind farm buildings is well worth a detour if only for its unusual 16th-century painted ceiling, which has clearly coloured heraldry, biblical texts and ornate floral and other decoration.

Off the A827, 2 miles (3 km) north-east
of Aberfeldy, a few miles east of Loch
Tay (map page 59)

APPLECROSS HIGHLAND

When Jacobite hopes of restoring Stuart kings collapsed in disarray at Culloden in 1746, and the infamous 'clearances' emptied the Highlands, old Scottish churches fell into disrepair and ruin. This is a typical example, with an old Celtic cross.

Reached by an atmospheric road off
the A896, to the north of Kyle of
Lochalsh (map page 59)

BIGGAR STRATHCLYDE

This small market town contains the Greenhill Covenanting Museum, housed in an old farmhouse re-erected on its present site; there are displays and relics relating to the illegal conventicles and other memories of three centuries ago.

The church, dating from 1545, is one of the last of the old-style 'collegiate' churches to be built before the Reformation.

In Biggar, on the A702, south-west of
Edinburgh (map page 58)

BRECHIN TAYSIDE

This parish church-cum-small cathedral contains many 13th-century details, such as the fine lancet work in the choir. Joined to it is a tall, lean round tower with a conical roof, which is of a kind found in Ireland. It tapers towards the top, and its windows and doors also have sloping sides.

Built in the 10th century as a refuge for the clergy against Viking raids, Brechin reflects the strong Irish influence of the early Celtic Church in Scotland.

Off the A94, 27 miles (43 km) north of
Dundee (map page 59)

CRIEFF TAYSIDE
TULLIBARDINE CHAPEL

Dating from around 1500 and little changed from pre-Reformation days, the church at Crieff has a typical military look with stone rubblework and stepped gables.

Churches in the days of clan warfare often had strong crenellated towers, hefty stone-slab roofs and other defensive features.

To the north of the A823, south-east of
Muthill (map page 59)

◆

CULLEN GRAMPIAN
AULD KIRK

A 16th-century church with Scottish features such as a sacrament house (an ornate wall recess for vessels) and a laird's loft (a gallery reserved for a local family). Some lofts had suites of rooms and other comforts; this example has fine carved panels.

On the A98, about 20 miles (32 km) east
of Elgin (map page 59)

◆

KIRKWALL ORKNEY
ST MAGNUS

Once a cathedral, now a parish church, its handsome uncluttered nave makes this Norman building seem larger than it is. The proportions are massive, but noble (the interior is best viewed from the west end), and they are not spoiled with too much decoration. The fine west

doorways with unusual rays of yellowish and red stone are later additions to this fine church.

In the centre of Kirkwall, on Mainland
in the Orkney Islands (map page 59)

◆

LEUCHARS FIFE

The parish church here dominates this sizeable village. It contains, in the chancel and rounded apse, plenty of typical 12th-century work, including chevron decoration and grotesque carved corbel heads.

5 miles (8 km) to the north-west of St
Andrews, off the A919 (map page 59)

◆

RODEL WESTERN ISLES
ST CLEMENTS

A solid, simple 16th-century church with tombs of MacLeod chieftains in jet-black stone glittering with quartz. The carvings echo early Celtic motifs and there is a pagan 'sheela-na-gig' fertility figure on the south wall.

In Rodel township, at the southern end
of Harris in the Western Isles
(map page 59)

◆

Glossary of Architectural Terms

abacus flat slab on top of a capital

aisle side passage to nave, separated from it by an arcade

altar a raised consecrated slab, replaced by a communion table in the Reformation, but often reinstated afterwards

ambulatory curved aisle around an apse

apse vaulted round or polygonal eastern end to church or chancel

arcade row of pillars carrying arches; a 'blind arcade' is merely decorative, with the arches being filled in

arch rounded or pointed head to an opening

ashlar smoothed, well-fitted stone blocks

auditory square classical plan of church

baldacchino an ornate classical canopy

ballflower Decorated petal ornament

Baroque ornate classical style

basilica Roman civic building copied in early church plans

battlement castle-like decoration to wall top

beakhead Norman decoration

belfry a bell tower; the part with bells

bellcote a roof support for bells

boss roof (ceiling) stud, often decorative

brass commemorative metal sheeting set into a ledger stone in floor or wall

broach junction of spire and tower

buttress projecting wall support; 'flying buttress' – its masonry separated from wall

cable decoration echoing twisted cord

capital (decorative) top of pillar (pier) enlarged for the springing of an arch

cell room or unit (nave, chancel) of early church building

chancel east end of church with the altar

chantry privately endowed altar; hence 'chantry chapel' holding such an altar

chapel enclosed area with its own altar often at the (eastern) end of an aisle or end of transept; St Mary is often commemorated in a 'Lady Chapel'

charnel house store for graveyard bones

chevron Norman zigzag decoration

choir feature of monastic, collegiate and cathedral churches, and adopted by Victorians

church building for public worship; as important for its sanctified churchyard

classical based on Greek and Roman style

clerestory top level of nave walls with windows

cloister covered arcade outside the building

column classical pillar

communion table replacement for the altar in churches in Reformation times

corbel block projecting from wall to support roof or other timbering; sometimes quaintly carved

cornice ornamental band at top of wall

crocket decorative knob of Decorated Gothic

cross Christian emblem, used symbolically – for example, preaching, wayside, churchyard and other wooden or stone crosses; as a token of the consecration of altar or church; as a pilgrim's mark etc

crossing intersection of side transepts with the main nave-chancel body of the church

cruciform cross-shaped church plan with transepts

crypt underfloor chamber, usually below chancel

cupola spherical roof of classical style

cusp inwardly projecting point of, for example, a trefoil

Decorated a Gothic style

dogtooth Early English starlike decoration

Doom wall painting of the Last Judgement

door often an antique feature of a church, with notable timbering, ironwork, sanctuary ring

doorway important part of early churches

dormer roof window

dripstone (arched) ledge to divert dripping rain

Early English an early Gothic style

Easter Sepulchre a niche in chancel wall which represents Christ's tomb

effigy depiction of dead, of interest as it shows clothing and armour of the time

fan vaulting (*see vault*)

flushwork walling of cut flints, often (decoratively) set chequered with stone panels

foil decorative lobed circle (for example, quatrefoil)

font bowl for baptism, usually of carved stone; often with a 'font cover' to protect the water

gable triangular wall ending to roof

gallery 1) Georgian addition to west end of nave, seating musicians; 2) upper storey of aisle

gargoyle waterspout, often grotesquely carved

Gothic the 'pointed arch' styles

graffiti informal scratched designs, figures

hammer-beam roof timbering

hatchment Georgian heraldic funeral board

herring-bone zigzag setting of wall stones

hood mould (*see dripstone*)

Jacobean of 17th-century style (of James I)

jamb vertical side post of doorway

Lady Chapel (*see chapel*)

lancet slender, pointed Early English window

Laudian rails communion rails around altar

lectern 'desk' (perhaps in eagle shape) from which the lesson is read

light 1) ventilation opening in spire; 2) window; 3) that part of window rising between mullions

linenfold panelling cut to imitate hanging cloth

lintel horizontal capping of door or window

long-and-short work (*see quoin*)

lych gate churchyard gate

mason's mark scratched token of medieval mason

Mass pre-Reformation (Catholic) communion

Mass dial simple sundial showing times of Mass

minster originally a Saxon 'mother church' but later sometimes rebuilt and enlarged

misericord perching bracket of tip-up choir seat

moulding decorative shaping, and especially of the steplike cut-away of arch

mullion vertical (stone) bar of window

nailhead pyramidal Early English ornament

narthex elaborate porch with chapel(s) at the western end of Saxon church

nave the main (i.e. the congregation's) part of the church

Norman a version of Romanesque architecture

ogee 'S'-curved: with convex-concave curve

oratory very early chapel, often monastic

order 1) retreating 'step' of an arch; 2) category of classical architecture

ossuary (*see charnel house*)

Palladian an architectural style influenced by the buildings of Andrea Palladio

parapet (battlemented) top of nave or tower

parclose screen or railing around a tomb, or shutting off a chapel

parvise room above a porch

pediment low gable over classical portico

peel (pele) tower defensive or refuge tower

Perpendicular the late Gothic style

pew seating for congregation

pier solid masonry leg supporting arches, often called a 'pillar' especially when slender; either simply round or polygonal, or clustered

pilaster vertical 'matchstick' decoration on a wall, perhaps to retain plastered wall surfacing

pillar (*see pier*)

pinnacle ornamental end spike of spire, buttress

piscina wall basin by altar for washing vessels

plasterwork decorative contoured plastering

plate the stone between tops of lancet windows, later cut to evolve into decorative tracery

plinth projecting base of wall or pillar (pier)

poppyhead erect, decorative end to a pew

porch grandiose doorway of many uses

portal/portico classical 'temple' entrance

porticus side chapel(s) of Saxon churches

pulpit raised stand from which sermon is given; sometimes with 'decks' of seating below

quoin strengthened cornering; Saxon buildings have distinctive 'long-and-short work'

reredos carved (painted) panel(s) behind altar

restored (of church) renewed in part or whole by Victorians in 'correct' Gothic style

rococo very ornately developed classical style

roll semicircular decorative band or retreating 'step', i.e. 'roll moulding' of an arch

Romanesque pre-Gothic style with round arches

rood depiction of Christ on the cross, on a wall or (later) carved and placed on a 'rood beam' crossing the chancel arch. This beam was later backed by a 'rood loft' for musicians and choir, which was reached by a 'rood stair' cut into the arch pillar. Below the beam was the carved and coloured 'rood screen' separating chancel and nave

roof externally of thatch, slate, tile etc; and internally with timbering either exposed or behind boarding. In classical churches the flat boarding is often decorated with plasterwork

sacristy storage room for vestments, vessels

sanctuary 1) setting of altar (i.e. part or whole of chancel); 2) immunity from persecution, hence 'sanctuary ring' grasped or knocked for entrance

Saxon pre-Conquest Romanesque architecture

scratch dial simple sundial (for example, Mass dial)

screen (often decorative) barrier in a church

sedilia (usually three) seats for officiating priests in the south wall of the chancel

shaft (slender) pillar perhaps 'tied' to another

shingle (spire) roofing of flat wooden pieces

sill horizontal beam or stone ledge at bottom of a wall or window, for example

spire pointed cap to tower

splay cut-away of wall alongside window

springing base point of arch; where it begins to curve away from the vertical pillar

squint window cut in wall to allow view of altar

stalls rows of (chancel) seating, especially for the choir

steeple tall tower, spire, or tower-plus-spire

stiff-leaf stylized Early English foliage

stilted (an arch) springing some way above the capital

stoup stone bowl for sanctified water

string course decorative lip of stone along a wall, perhaps once edging plaster (*see pilaster*)

stucco (classical style) ornamental plasterwork

swag decorative festoon

tester sounding board projecting above pulpit

tomb burial edifice; a 'chest tomb' is a box-like memorial raised above the burial

tracery intersecting, decorative stonework of a window

transept side arm of cruciform church

Transitional earliest form of Gothic style

transom horizontal window bar (*see mullion*)

Tudor as well as a political period this is a developed Perpendicular style of, for example, doorway, window

tympanum area between the door top (lintel) and the arch above

vault curved stone ceiling; a 'fan vault' is characteristic of the finest Perpendicular architecture

wall painting once an important part of any church, most often on nave, chancel walls

waterleaf broad-leaf Early English ornament

windows by their style these give an indication of their date

Index

Acknowledgements

◆

The photographs in *Country Churches* were supplied by the photographers and
agencies listed below:

AA Photolibrary pp. 2, 8, 12, 15, 23, 27, 28, 31, 35, 37, 38, 46, 51, 54, 60, 64,
66–7, 72, 75, 80, 83, 89, 90, 96, 99, 109, 112, 114, 124, 146, 148
Dennis Baldry p. 119
Jeffrey Beazley pp. 85, 128
John Bethell pp. 13, 21, 41, 43, 87, 100, 134, 137, 140
Janet & Colin Bord/Wales Scene pp. 16, 102, 122, 126
John Heseltine pp. 18, 49
Images Colour Library/Derry Brabbs pp. 71, 88 (and front cover), 106, 143
Janette Widdows p. 95

The line drawings are by Lyn Cawley, and the church illustrations in the
gazetteer are by Sheilagh Noble.

The maps on pp. 56–9 were drawn by John Gilkes.